Advanced St
for Marketin

Innovative Ways to Boost Your Art Career

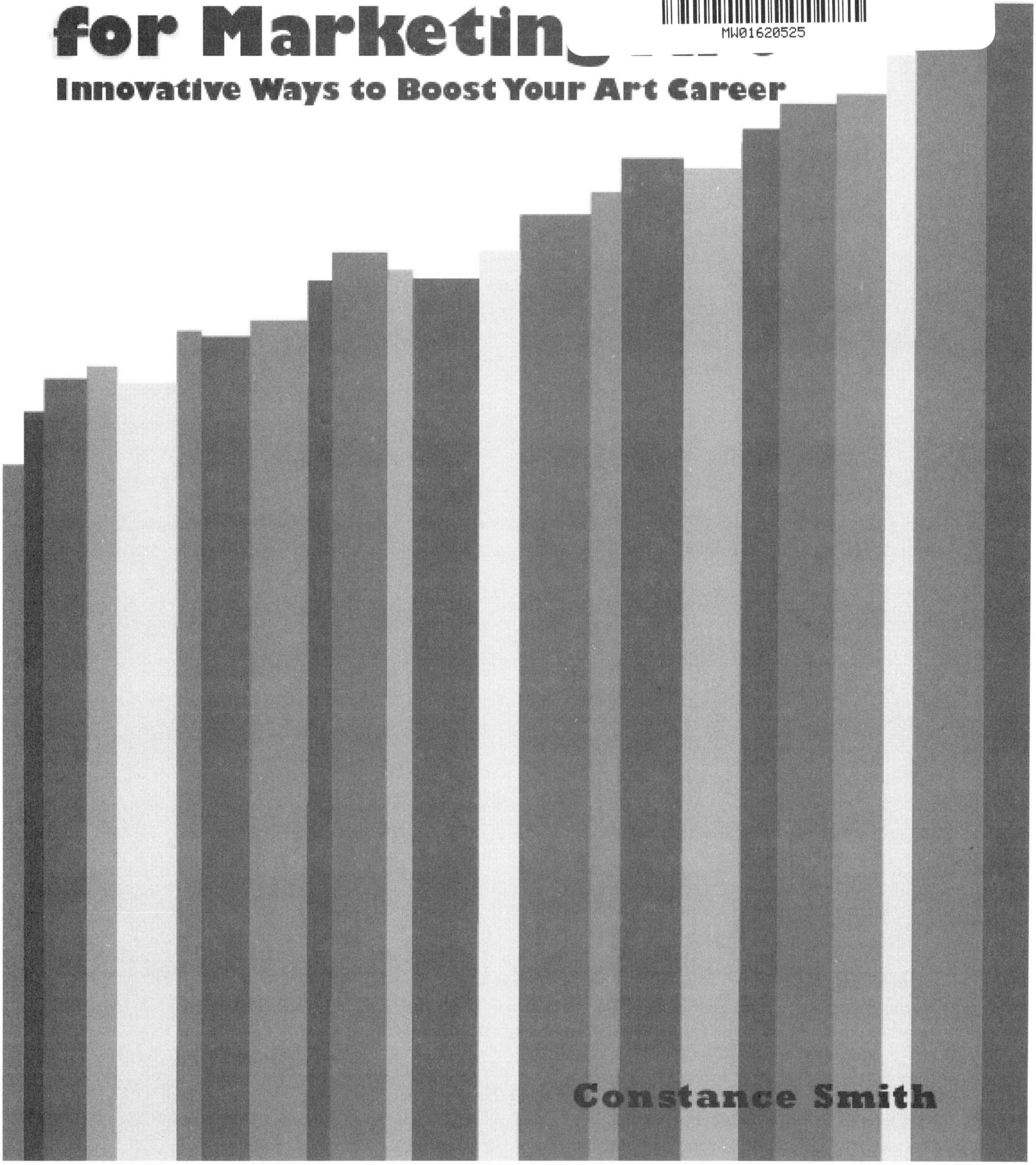

Constance Smith

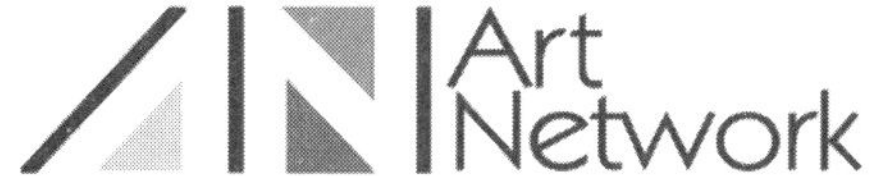

Advanced Strategies for Marketing Art,
Innovative Ways to Boost Your Art Career

First Edition March 2011

Cover design by Laura Ottina Davis

Published by ArtNetwork, 10647 Red Dog Rd, Nevada City, CA 95959 530/478-0920
www.artmarketing.com info@artmarketing.com

ArtNetwork was created in 1986 with the idea of teaching fine artists how to earn a living from selling their art.

Publisher's Cataloging-in-Publication Data

Smith, Constance, 1949-

Advanced strategies for marketing art : innovative ways to boost your art career / by Constance Smith.

p. cm.

ISBN: 978-0-940899-55-1

1. Art—Marketing. 2. Art—Economic aspects. I. Title.

HF5415.1265 .S613 2011

706.8—dc22

Library of Congress Control Number: 2010943019

Printed and bound in the United States of America

Distributed to the trade in the United States by Consortium Book Sales and Distribution

Introduction

Artists often have a thing about the word "business." It frightens them. They might think that marketing is a magic formula that you are taught in Harvard Business School. As they begin to market their art, however, they find out that creating a business is basically using common sense, perhaps combined with a positive attitude and innovative ideas. Taking risks and trying unconventional approaches is part of the mix.

Composing this book has been an organic process. I have been conversing with artists for over 25 years. Experiences—notes and oral memories—were gathered and started to spill forth. This book is filled with so many ideas that it might even overwhelm you. Take one chapter at a time and develop your own ideas around the topics covered.

Trial and error is a necessity in any business. In this book you will find many ideas to start on your own unique path. The advanced marketing techniques you will encounter within are meant to inspire each one of you to discover your own personal approach to marketing.

As you proceed, you will gain knowledge, experience, confidence and success. Success follows entrepeneurs who overcome their fears and roadblocks. I hope this book will guide you in that direction.

Getting Started

The fact that you have this book in your hands tells me that you have decided to talk the talk and walk the walk of marketing your art.

If this is the first art marketing book you've picked up to read, you'll be missing a lot of necessary basics: You need to read *Art Marketing 101* (www.artmarketing.com), which covers business basics such as record keeping, legal protection, pricing, resumes, and how to create a marketing plan for your business. When you start any business, you must understand your particular industry's standards and rules. Once you've gotten all the basics in order, you'll be ready to rip through the information in this book.

This advanced book was written to guide artists in building their art business; help them surmount brick walls. This advanced book assumes you've already (1) created art for awhile and have (2) started to think about your business manifesto (mission statement).

It is impossible, even with great effort and talent, to guarantee a major career. Major artists emerge as a result of a confluence of factors. It is possible, however, to guarantee a career that allows you to use the artwork you've created as a major source of income. To do this, most artists will have to change the way they think about the art world and their role in it. The more determined the effort, the longer the endeavor, the better the chances of success.

If you can dedicate four to eight hours a week to marketing for a year, you will have worked for one to two-and-a-half months on marketing for the year! Compared to your previous sporadic attempts, this consistent goal-induced plan will get you a lot further. Ten to 20 hours a week of smart marketing will take you even further.

You will accomplish the most if you are completely honest and straightforward with yourself while you study this book. Try to see your personal strengths and weaknesses with clarity.

If you are at a difficult juncture in your personal life, perhaps it would be better to put this book down for awhile, and come to it later with a fresh emotional outlook. Having too much on your plate makes it easier to fail. Don't defeat your will in this manner.

This book is the beginning of finding solutions to your marketing problems. It will enable you to analyze your situation and develop a personalized approach to your business and career. To help stay on track:

- Keep all your ideas, notes and thoughts on marketing in one place.
- Writing down facts will give you a better idea of where you are in your career as well as where you want to land.

Use this book as a workbook; don't fret about marking up this book. Answer the questions that are asked in the book; fill in the blanks. Skipping answers will only delay your progress. There are no shortcuts to success. Commit yourself totally and sign the following contract with yourself.

Contract with Self

I, ________________________________, understand that I am going to work diligently so that I can progress with my career as a fine artist. I also understand that there will be barriers, both psychological and emotional, that I will have to attempt to break through. I know it is possible and therefore wish to progress to the highest of my capabilities.

Table of Contents

Chapter 1 Inspiration

The path . . . 10
Dreaming . . . 13
Finding your voice . . . 17
A mission statement . . . 18
Coaches . . . 20
Professional assistance . . . 22
12 ways to prosper in a down economy . . . 23
Overwhelm . . . 26

Chapter 2 The Internet

Using the Internet . . . 28
Exhibiting art online . . . 29

Chapter 3 Entering the Art Market

Setting the stage . . . 32
Target market . . . 33
Competitors . . . 34
The art of the telephone . . . 35
10 ways to expand your clientele . . . 39

Chapter 4 Sales Techniques

Learning to sell . . . 42
Handling objections . . . 44
Follow-up . . . 47
A science to purchasing . . . 48
Leasing art . . . 49
Patron programs . . . 50
Gift certificates . . . 52

Chapter 5 Promotional pieces

Direct mail . . . 56
Competent design . . . 58
Postcards . . . 59
Mailing lists . . . 61
E-newsletters . . . 64

CHAPTER 6 ADVERTISING

Ad placement 66
Artist directories 68

CHAPTER 7 PUBLIC ART

Publicly-funded programs 70
Working with nonprofits 76
Museums 81

CHAPTER 8 REPS AND CONSULTANTS

Art reps 86
Art consultants 87
Approaching art consultants 90
Set decorators 93
Private collectors 95

CHAPTER 9 GALLERIES

The gallery scene 98
The gallery search 99
Meeting with a gallery owner 103
Studio visits 106
Working with a gallery 107
Legalities 108
University galleries 112
Rental galleries 113
Co-op galleries 114

CHAPTER 10 ART PLACEMENT IN BUSINESSES

The corporate market 116
Healthcare settings 119
Hotels 121
Wineries 122
Religious organizations 123
Small businesses 124
Interior designers 125
Architects 126
Real estate 127
Publishing and licensing 128

Chapter 11 The Portrait Market

Getting a commission . . . 130
Initial consultation . . . 131
First meeting . . . 133
Sessions . . . 135
The unveiling . . . 136
Legal aspects . . . 137
Resources . . . 139
Pet portraits . . . 140

Chapter 12 Art Competitions

Entering competitions . . . 142
Locating competitions . . . 144

Chapter 13 Art Fairs and Shows

Outdoor art fairs . . . 146
Art trade shows . . . 151
Open studio shows . . . 153

Chapter 14 Funding

Grants . . . 160
Grant givers . . . 164
Residencies . . . 165
Moonlighting . . . 168

Chapter 15 Workshops and Travel

Developing a workshop . . . 170
Speaking at a conference . . . 175
Attending an art workshop . . . 177
Art travel . . . 178

Chapter 1

Inspiration

The path

Dreaming

Finding your voice

A mission statement

Coaches

Professional assistance

12 ways to prosper in a down economy

Overwhelm

A journey of a thousand miles begins with a single step.
Confucius

THE PATH

Know what you're aiming for and why. Then go for it!

Hooray! You've decided that it's time to start the process of marketing and selling your artwork seriously. Perhaps you have made some attempts previously, but not with a specific goal in mind. You've now realized that you need a business plan. This book will help you brainstorm new ideas to get a great plan in order. Reading *Art Marketing 101* as preparation for this advanced marketing book is a prerequisite to helping you make the most of your new knowledge.

SUCCESS

Think about the idea of success, particularly pertaining to your art career. Some people measure success by the amount of money they make. Others consider that success is being free from the nine-to-five grind. Whatever your definition of success, with a strong and persistent aim, it is possible to obtain it. By studying your motivation, you will understand how to go for complete success.

THE FIRST STEP

- Identify what you personally consider business success to be. Is it helping humanity, expressing yourself creatively or politically, making money at what you enjoy doing, volunteering for a cause, painting a canvas?
- Are you willing to make concessions to reach success? If so, what are they? Are you willing to work hard, overcome rejections, spend less time with your family?
- Is success to you being a millionaire or living in middle-class comfort?

Write down below what you personally consider success. Mull it over for a time; it will probably develop and change.

STRETCH YOUR MIND

Have you ever imagined yourself to be a successful artist, receiving a bit of fame, enjoying selling a painting, not having to worry about where your next loaf of bread will come from? Have you ever envisioned a new studio in your back lot, large enough to store and organize all your equipment, comfortable in winter and summer, with northern windows? If you have not envisioned these or similar scenarios, you need to. You must envision your version of what a successful art career is in order to accomplish it.

Silent viewing. I personally do silent viewing while soaking in a hot bathtub. When the body relaxes, you can see clues within your mind's eye of new ways to deal with various aspects of your life. Some people meditate in a yoga position.

Some heed nighttime dreams. Listen to your intuition, and the stories and scenes it brings forth, and it will lead you to your personal and business success.

Journaling. Writing helps us to see beneath the surface that which otherwise might remain hidden. It's important to finish the tasks assigned in this book and write down your thoughts. It will bring you to your inner mission, as well as help to ground you.

Comfort zone. Attempt to understand something beyond your normal realm. This could be scientific, computer-related, intellectual, or about another artist's philosophy that varies from your own. Such attempts expand you. Start taking some risks.

Allow for impulsiveness. It's necessary to have a schedule, but don't schedule every minute of your day. Allow for impulsive (often intuitive) activities, and serendipitous things often happen.

Instead of getting disappointed when there's a setback, consider how much this incident will matter in five or ten years. This will give you some perspective.

VISUALIZE SUCCESS

You need to be able to visualize a scene in order to get there eventually. I used to say, "I can't paint." I had tried once but wasn't happy with the result. For 20 years after that, I never picked up a paint brush. When I finally tried painting again, I realized I could paint. I certainly had my own style, but I could paint. Within nine months I had done a self portrait, several other portraits, and many other pieces that still hang on my walls. I realized I didn't need to be afraid of my style of expression. I had to confront it. I had to mature. I had to accept.

In the same way, you must visualize success with your marketing and sales.

RESISTANCE TO SUCCESS

Amazingly enough, you can start attracting people and situations to bring you the particular success you want. It's your job to not reject them when they appear. Believe it or not, when you finally start receiving what you desire, there will be some resistance. It often comes in the form of anger, frustration at particular people (who have helped you arrive at success), and other negative reactions. It's amazing how we can resist what's good for us! Having your aims written down will help you realize what your negative instincts are trying to deter.

FACTORS TO SUCCESS

Take your business seriously

Call yourself an artist; if you don't, no one will.
Study your personal roadblocks.
Know how rejection affects you and be ready when it "attacks."

Educate yourself

Learn the basic legal rights of an artist.
Find an artist you admire; imitate her professionalism.
Take advantage of your local art resources: art council, art organizations.

Price right

Study the market before you begin to sell.
Offer a guarantee: Make customers feel safe about purchasing from you.

Exposure equals success

Get your work out there; exhibit; be seen.
Remind your clients you exist with postcards and e-mails.
Make your web site better than others; tell your story.

Provide a service

Give more service than "the artist next door."
Make it easy to buy: a web site, open studio hours, posted prices.
Offer extras: hanging work, delivery.

Provide what your customers want

Quality products and quality service will bring repeat customers.

Look and be professional

Let customers know you're in business for the long haul.
Stay organized; know who bought what.

Create a marketing plan

Create a five-year marketing plan; update it biannually.
Create a one-year plan; update it monthly.

Think outside the box

Don't put all your eggs in one basket. Create a variety of venues to sell in: studio shows, outdoor shows, exhibits, salons with other artists.

Don't give up

Keep on truckin': Every entrepreneur has ups and downs.

Realities can come true via an inspirational dream. Let's consider what your long-term "dreams" are. We'll go into the depths of who you are in order to see what you truly desire in the area of art. When you spend time inside your quiet self, you will be able to see your aspirations more clearly. By seeing and acknowledging them, you set them in motion. It sounds a little like voodoo, and for most people it is.

DREAM EXERCISE

Try the following exercise; make it a bi-weekly habit; you will soon find magic coming your way.

Using a spiral notebook, leaving pages available for future weeks, write down your passions regarding your art career—not your aims, but your wildest dreams. If you could have anything you wanted regarding your art career, what would you choose? Write this in private so no one will critique you.

Don't hold anything back. Don't be afraid that you won't achieve your wildest dreams. Shoot for the moon. We've been told so often that it's selfish to think like that, so we hold back and don't allow our wishes even to be voiced. Do this exercise for two or more months, listing at least nine "wild" dreams relating to your art career. Be sure to spend some quiet time with yourself before you write these down. A muddled mind could lead you astray. After you fill this list out every other week, let it rest. Do not dwell on it. Date and keep all your lists. When time has passed, look at the lists and analyze.

WILD DREAMS
WEEK _____

1. ______________________________
2. ______________________________
3. ______________________________
4. ______________________________
5. ______________________________
6. ______________________________
7. ______________________________
8. ______________________________
9. ______________________________

- Which wild dreams come up again and again on the list?
- What has happened since you wrote down these off-the-wall dreams? Has anything "dropped' into your life that shows you might be drawing these dreams into being?

DREAMING

Relaxing into the moment can become the most important factor in success.

Think towards your dreams, passions and desires, not away from them.

INTENDING

Remember that the clearer you can be in describing your passion, dream or aim, the more likely you will receive exactly what you are asking for. You are not trying or hoping for these dreams to come true; you are intending for them to happen with efforts on your part that are deemed necessary.

You will have learned to empower yourself to new heights and can apply this type of thinking and acting—intending—to all parts of your life. It becomes a way of life, a way you can't turn back from. You will start getting what you want out of life—what you were sent here for.

Deal with your goals as your intent, and they will occur.

- Visualize the outcome you intend for your wild dreams. If you can't visualize something, then it probably won't occur.
- List the biggest challenges in reaching your wildest dreams.

  ____

  ____

- Organize on a calendar (download a weekly, monthly and annual calendar at www.artmarketing.com/downloads.html) the steps you need to take to accomplish one of your wild dreams. Set a firm deadline for each phase. Make it realistic. Anticipate delays; often, it takes twice as long and costs twice as much as anticipated—a formidable law of the universe.

BLOSSOMING

Something that is blossoming already has roots. The seed has sprouted and now it's about to bloom and change into a different creature. Each time you allow something new to come into your life—a new dream—you must give it due space or it will not blossom to its full potential. Sometimes other passions will have to be put on hold in order to accommodate fulfilling the newest dream.

MOTIVATING

Discern what motivates you. What methods work to get you to your destination? Gurus and teachers can give you clues to your personal path (see pages 20-22).

Some days, it's harder than others to motivate yourself. Hanging in the air are the remains of . . . well, often we don't even know! So we just tread through the hours and keep our head up. Perhaps these more difficult times are when we don't believe in ourself; inner strength is wavering.

- Are you doing activities you don't really want to do?
- Is it just the ebb and tide, natural to all existence?

Pleasing

Whom are we trying to please, anyway? Ask yourself this. You'll see that many times we are doing something to please someone else: a parent, a potential mate, society, a professor, a peer, an audience, you name it—maybe even a dog!

This is not what you want to do. Be selfish. Please yourself. You'll find that by doing this, you will begin to receive what you desire. But you must first know exactly what it is you desire—no wishy-washy here.

- Being selfish is okay as long as you are not stepping on anyone's toes.
- You will get what you ask for, so be ready. If you ask to become "famous," are you truly ready for celebrity—more criticism than ever, no privacy and all that it entails? Know what you want, be clear, and know you can alter your intentions as you learn.
- There is an abundance of everything. You are not in competition with anyone.
- Your thoughts create your world.

Success for artists is about relationships. You have to gain access to people's emotions and keep them invigorated.

Another exercise

Take the one dream that is strongest from your list of wild dreams. You are going to use that as your basis in this exercise.

Start elaborating on what you imagine this dream to entail. Who are the characters who play a part? Let's say that one of your dreams is to be a professional artist who enjoys total freedom of creation and success in marketing. Can you envision the studio you would be working in? Write down in detail its description. Write down your attitude, words people are saying, any detail you can pick out. Make this vision very specific and real in your mind's eye. Create a plot, a story.

This is not meant to be a quick exercise. Do not rush through it, or it will be of no use. This could turn out to be one of the most important exercises for marketing: attempting to improve your inner vision.

Concentrate on this particular dream for a period of time: every day for a month or more. Put big notes on your bathroom mirror, kitchen refrigerator and office computer as a reminder to bring this dream into your life. You will see that you begin to attract its manifestation. Keep a close watch on all your thoughts while "intending" your new dream. Resistances will come in. Doubts are natural; don't listen to them. They have been programmed into you through society, your family, your religion. Worst-case scenarios inevitably seem to pop into the mind. It is your job to not believe them. Listen only to ideas that lead to your dream.

"Unfolding" is discovering your genius. You didn't know you were a genius? Everyone has the potential to be a genius.

MAKING IT

Write down in a few words where you'd like to be in five years.

____

____

Incorporate the above information in your five-year plan (see more about marketing plans in *Art Marketing 101*).

Create your reality; don't just meander to an indefinite place. If it is a true passion and innate to your being, it will begin to happen. The end result might not be exactly as you originally pictured, but this is not the aim. The aim is to follow the cues and adapt as necessary.

FINDING YOUR VOICE

Your paintings should not exist solely as individual entities, but as songs from a musical—each relating to and expanding on the others.

A voice is the style—including technique and medium—that defines your artwork. It is distinct, recognizable.

- If we had 20 photos from two artists, would we be able to separate them into two stacks of 10, one for each artist? If viewers cannot distinguish a definite style for each artist, then there is no clear voice from that artist.

The energy that you bring to your creativity becomes your voice. Your voice carries into all your life but is especially visible through the product of your creativity. It is powerful and ever-looming. Having a voice goes hand in hand with the development of a heart. We are born with a heart, but in order to use it to its full capacity, we need to develop it.

A common mistake is to be too random in creation of style, although it is fine to experiment—in fact, one must. To be marketable, an artist must have a definite personal style—a vision that sets him apart from everyone else. This style most often takes artists years to develop, slowly morphing from practice to presentation.

Body of work

Artists marketing their work must have a substantial body of work available for sale—at least 20 or more pieces that meet the standard of quality you have set for yourself. These pieces must have a consistent, cohesive style—your voice—with a well-defined sense of direction.

Analysis

Haven't found your voice? Don't fret. In fact, you must do the opposite of fret. You must "relax into" your voice—it is the only way to find it. It comes naturally, sometimes developing over a long haul, sometimes seeming to appear suddenly. All the emotional, psychological and practical attempts you make take you toward your voice. Your voice is you.

Finding this voice can take years. Until you personally feel you have found your voice, it is best to not market your art.

Creativity

The process of creating is very important to the psyche. Whether you are famous or popular or sell your work doesn't matter to the psyche. Creating is a constant necessity for an artist. Reading biographies of well-known artists—Duchamp, Nicholson, Rothko—will show you they are continually seeking, seeking, seeking something new, unknown to them. So you, too, in your processing, will go through something similar. It is actually not too different from what any entrepreneur goes through in the process of building a company: ever changing, continually growing.

A MISSION STATEMENT

A mission statement is a proclamation of purpose.

In *Art Marketing 101* we discussed writing an artist statement. An artist statement is an integral part of an artist's marketing process. It captures your philosophy so your clients can better understand your artwork.

Another type of statement that will help you focus your business aims is a "mission statement." Corporations and entrepreneurs create this type of statement so potential clients will understand their goals and purpose.

A mission statement usually includes your company's function, products and services you provide, why you exist—values and beliefs, competitive advantages, goals and philosophies, value system, behavioral standards. Creating a mission statement helps you understand your motivation, which in turn helps make your aims become a reality. When you have begun to delve into some of the questions posed below, you will have the basis for creating your mission statement.

Use the process of creating your mission statement as a learning tool for yourself. When you go astray, are down, or lost in a muddle, reviewing this statement can help you refocus on what your aim was when you were in a more enlightened state.

BRAINSTORMING

Why am I an artist?
What do critics say about my work?
Define success for myself at this point in my life.
List expectations that I have for my art career.
List five people I admire and two adjectives to describe them.
What artists do I most admire?
List five traits in myself as an adult that I admire.
Define my artistic passions.
What are the strong points of my artwork?
What are the weak points of my artwork?
How has my art changed in the last two years?
What are my personal marketing strengths?
What are my personal marketing weaknesses?
In what ways have I practiced persistence and perseverance?
What risks have I taken to advance my career?
In what ways have I made a total commitment to my art career?
How have I used a rejection to my advantage?
Why do I want to sell my art?
What's my primary aim in establishing this business?
How do I solve a customer's problem?
Who are my clients?
What do my clients need?

ONLINE RESOURCES

- www.pommfineart.com/artist_mission_statement.shtml
- www.susanmorrison.com, then "about Susan"
- www.waynesrealisticproducts.com/mission.html
- www.online-business-plans.com, then Sept 2004 newsletter

TIPS

- Note your statement in the present tense—what you are trying to accomplish now.
- Don't fret about being "perfect"—there is no perfect.
- The mission statement should not be clever or catchy, just accurate.
- This statement is a work in progress.
- Don't rush the process.

Whether you think you can or think you can't, you're right.
Henry Ford

COACHES

One of my favorite artists, along with his philosophy, is Mark Kostabi. He has written several books. My favorite is *Conversations with Kostabi* in which he expounds on his art marketing theories. Chapter Six is entitled *How to Become Rich and Famous*. www.artnet.com/magazineus/features/kostabi/kostabi1-20-06.asp

Account execs at large firms use life coaches to help them reach both their business and personal goals. It's a great idea for an emerging artist to follow this trend.

An artist coach assists artists, sometimes on a one-time basis, with aspects of their career: creating a marketing plan, suggesting venues or geographic areas for sales, organizing their business, brainstorming new ideas for marketing, critiquing artwork. Coaches give private consultations and also conduct seminars and workshops.

WHY COACHING WORKS

- Coaches hold students accountable.
- Coaches are impartial.
- Coaches help you set goals, get organized, and manage your time; they also provide support and give advice in business decisions.

ARTIST COACHES

Art Tech Publishing www.theartistnotebook.com

Alan Bamberger www.artbusiness.com

Barbara Bowen www.gatewaystocreativity.com

Jamie Brunson www.jamiebrunson.com/coaching.html

Katherine Carter www.ktcassoc.com

Paul Cundiff www.kentuckyartists.com/artmarketing

Margaret Danielak www.danielakart.com

Susan Ann Darley www.empoweringartists.com

Aletta de Wal www.artistcareertraining.com

Susan Fader www.myartmarketingcoach.com

Wendy Froshay www.theartmentor.com

Gloria Gales www.thebusinessofart.com

Geoffrey Gorman www.artistcube.com (See article page 92)

Kathy Gulrich www.smartbusinesscoaching.com

Jason Horejs www.xanadugallery.com (See article page 111)

Robert Maniscalco www.maniscalcogallery.com/coaching.htm

Joanne Mattera www.joannemattera.blogspot.com

Andre Milan www.artistsconsult.com

Renee Phillips www.renee-phillips.com

Elisa Pritzker www.pritzkerstudio.com

Heather Rothnie www.yourartcopilot.com

Alyson Stanfield www.artbizcoach.com (See article page 21)

William Torphy Fine Arts www.torphyart.com

Marcel Wah www.wahfinearts.com

Sylvia White www.artadvice.com (See article pages 101-102)

Martha Zlatar www.artmatch-coach.com

Web sites

Browse these sites for more info to help you toward business success.

www.bob-baker.com - Articles on marketing and promotion

www.art-support.com - Portfolio guidelines, copyright info and more

www.wildlife-fantasy.com - Articles to help other artists promote their site

www.thethrivingartist.com/resources - Great references

Treat yourself and your with respect.

Breakfast Circle

If you're not networking with other fine artists who are marketing their artwork, you are missing out on an important element leading to success. An artist recently told me about her local (Soho, NY) "Artist Breakfast Circle." Once a week from 7:30-8:30 am, about 15-25 artists meet at a coffee shop. The "meeting" is conducted in a very specific fashion—no one is allowed to ramble on and on; one artist is in charge of the meeting, keeping things under control. Marketing issues are brought up and briefly discussed. Those who want to get together afterwards do so on their own. It is thought-provoking and energizing—a real boost to everyone's marketing week.

PROFESSIONAL ASSISTANCE

Professional assistance and knowledge are constantly needed to keep yourself ahead of the crowd.

All business owners—even pro athletes worth millions—seek assistance in areas they need to improve. Follow their lead and keep up your education. Make professionalism a habit.

CONFERENCES AND SEMINARS

Art and Business Council of New York
www.artsandbusiness-ny.org/professional_development/namp/default.asp

Art Exposure Inc www.artexposureinc.com
Business and legal classes for artists in Baltimore

Artist in the Marketplace/AIM www.bronxmuseum.org/aim.html
The Bronx Museum of the Arts has a 12-week program on career management for artists—a great opportunity to learn more, become motivated, and network within the art community. Eighteen lucky artists are accepted into the program annually. Deadline for applying is mid-January.

BizArt Conferences www.bizartinfo.com
Conferences are held in Chicago, Seattle, Florida and more.

The Business of Art www.annbell.net/artbusinessclass.htm

Center for Education, Business and the Arts/CEBA www.cebakanecounty.org

Creative Chicago Expo www.chicagoartistsresource.org
Held annually; vendors, workshops and consultants exhibit at this free event

GYST www.bukst-ink.com

Indian Arts & Crafts Association www.iaca.com/?pageid=20

Klein Artist Works www.kleinartistsworks.com

Marketplace Empowerment for Artists/MEA
www.tremainefoundation.org/Content/Art_Programs.asp

New York Foundation for the Arts/NYFA
www.nyfa.org/level3.asp?id=660&fid=1&sid=76

SEA Conferences www.selfemploymentinthearts.com

smARTist Telesummit www.1shoppingcart.com/app/?af=703172
An annual online course that lasts 10 days

St Johns Cultural Art Center www.stjohnsculture.com

Success as an Artist www.thefrasergallery.com/seminars.html

12 WAYS TO PROSPER IN A DOWN ECONOMY

If you know you are in the business of marketing your art, then you will look at a down economy as another moment to explore new possibilities. You know you will sell, you will continue marketing and your business will survive. You continue because you must.

HAVE A PLAN

It is critical to update your marketing plan during a down economy. Changes will have to be made. Your plan will need to be reevaluated quarterly. Make sure your marketing plan has dollar amounts in it.

Most businesses fail before three years. If you don't give up before that time, you'll have made it a long way. If you are as good an artist as you claim to be, you must continue to believe in your work. Who else will if you don't? Consider your business a marathon, not a sprint.

USE THE INTERNET

Study what other artists are doing to survive. What new tactics are they using: lower prices, smaller pieces? What else? How are galleries continuing to survive?

Update your web site and make it appealing to new collectors. Plan e-mail blasts to your clients at opportune times.

HOOK UP WITH A NONPROFIT

Use your marketing savvy and come up with some good ideas to share with a nonprofit. Help them create a fundraiser. (See Chapter 6.) Make it a win-win situation; do something for them and they for you.

PRICING

People will spend only $100 for an artwork now, whereas previously they might have spent $500. Those who like to buy art still want to buy more, but their price line has changed. Accommodate them with wonderful, small pieces. Be innovative: Use wrapped canvases that don't need to be framed.

KEEP BRANDING

It's very important that you not lose your previous momentum. Let people know that you are still an artist, still in business and that you intend to be around beyond these rough times. If you must take a part-time job, that's okay. No one even needs to know.

Read *Branding Yourself Online* by Bob Baker.

Diversify

Is it time to start selling giclées or looking for a publisher or licensor? Should you teach an art course? Stretch yourself. Take a risk.

Network

Becoming an exhibiting artist means you can no longer hide in your studio. You will have to make efforts to network, contacting a variety of people in the art world (and beyond) on a weekly basis.

- Networking is a two-way situation—giving and receiving.
- Almost every civic community has networking groups—a Chamber of Commerce, for instance. They usually consist of business owners who meet once a month for cocktails to get to know each other. You can join these groups as an artist in business—no different from an accountant, dentist, or newspaper writer who has joined.
- Serving on a committee, such as at a local arts council or museum, is a great way to network and meet new people. Let them know, "I'm an artist."
- People generally prefer to patronize people they know. If you get to know them and they like your work, they might offer you a show at their house or refer you to a friend who is renovating.
- Don't be shy. When you pick up your drycleaning and pay your bill, hand them your business card. When anyone asks what you "do," have a business card to hand her—maybe even two so she can give one to a friend. Let everyone in your community know who you are and be proud of it. Pretty soon you will be famous!

Collaborate

Collaboration, especially if you are a loner or power-freak, is a great exercise. If you can truly get into it, the outcome will be exponential to your solo venture.

Get together with a few artists in your community who are still exposing their artwork. Come up with something as a group: a show, a mailer, classes. During difficult economic times, people look for inexpensive, lively venues where they can socialize. Perhaps it's time to open your home once a month for a collaborative home or studio show.

Go beyond

Dazzle your clients; do something special for them. Professionalism counts during tough economic times more than any other time. Answer the phone promptly, and be extra courteous and friendly. Do what's required, then go one step beyond.

SPEND LESS

Study your previous years' financial statements and see what you can cut back on expenditure-wise. When we have more monies flowing through, it's natural to spend more.

Create a budget for both your business and personal spending. Cutting in both areas will help to take off some pressure.

PR

Step up your PR efforts. Though PR can be time-consuming, the no-cost aspect makes it worthwhile. Read *Power Up with PR* (www.artmarketing.com) to educate yourself.

STAY IN CONTACT WITH THE 20%

Remember the 80/20 rule: 20% of your contacts purchase 80% of your work. Keep in touch with the 20%.

OVERWHELM

You are what you think you are.

At this point, do you feel overwhelmed? There's a lot to accomplish as you develop your business. Don't cling to overwhelm (though it will want to hang onto you). It creeps into everyone's day at some point. Fortunately, all states pass, and overwhelm will too.

- When you get overwhelmed with challenges, start breaking them down to smaller, more digestible tasks.
- Physically move. Do something rote: Straighten an unorganized garage, clean a messy studio, organize a desk. There is always something that you can "do" immediately to put a plan into action. Take one step at a time; put each step on your calendar so it becomes a "must do" activity.

PROJECTS

If you have more than three major projects going at the same time, it's probably too many. Make sure you don't agree to more responsibilities than you can handle. If your business is your number-one priority, you need to treat it as such. Make it a habit. When you are creating a new business, you must take risks and create new habits that head you toward your aim.

- Of the three major projects (and probably five minor ones) you have going, you must prioritize. Write this prioritization down on paper. Include all the necessary movements to accomplish the next step of each of these projects in your monthly and daily calendars.
- Make sure you know the goals of each project. If there is no benefit to a project, you will have no desire to complete it.

SELF-EMPLOYMENT

You've decided to sell your artwork and develop a business: You are a self-employed entrepreneur! Working for yourself will constantly remind you that success is determined more by your state of mind than by external events.

- You have become responsible for your artwork and communicating its value to your prospective clients.
- You are responsible for your daily state of mind: If you think things will go wrong, that will happen.
- Marketing becomes simple: Love what you do and be willing to share.
- Without action, nothing develops.
- Entrepreneurs learn from their mistakes; otherwise they will ultimately fail.

If you can be clear on exactly what you want to accomplish and then ask for it, you will most likely receive it. It's a cosmic law.

Chapter 2

The Internet

Using the Internet

Exhibiting art online

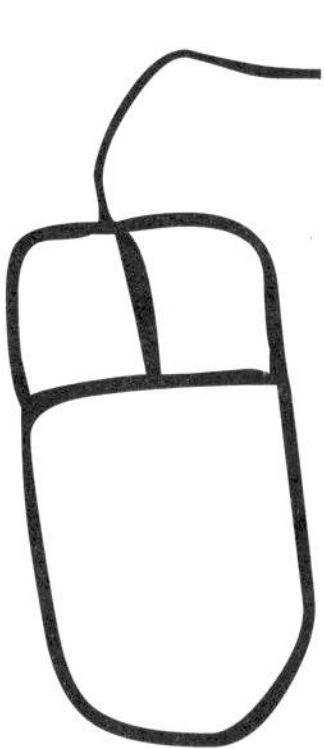

Being an artist is a way of being. It's not just what you produce.
Friedensreich Hundertwasser

USING THE INTERNET

Most of us, by now, know a bit about the Internet: how to send and reply to e-mail, how to research a trip we want to take, how to make a reservation, how to buy on Amazon. If, for some reason, you're not even that far along, it's time to settle down and get educated. A business cannot function well these days without its main representatives knowing how to use the Internet to their advantage.

INTERNET OPTIONS

The Internet is an amazing tool, and as a progressive business, you have to take advantage of it.

- **Communication.** E-mail is a must.
- **Transferring files.** There are possibilities for downloading files onto your own computer: clip art, software, music. You will also need to know how to create a PDF file.
- **Research.** You can do all kinds of research, both business and personal: Locate art consultants and interior designers who work with artists; see what styles they work with, and much more. You'll be able to study what other artists are creating, what they are charging and how they are marketing.
- **Banking.** Knowing how to bank online makes your life easier. You can verify cleared checks, see a bank balance, do transfers and more.
- **Selling art.** You can sell your art on eBay, Etsy, your personal web site or at an online gallery.
- **Social media.** Social media have swept the world in the last few years. Taking advantage of networking opportunities associated with social media can be great for your career.
- *Social Networking for Artists* www.artcalendar.com/article.asp?ID=203
- *How to Sell on Facebook* www.finearttips.com/category/blog/business-tips
- *To Tweet or Not to Tweet* www.artmarketing.com/ToTweet.html
- *Selling Your Art Online* www.northlightshop.com.
- *10 Steps to Getting your Sh*t Together* www.gyst-ink.com/blog/?p=28

EXHIBITING ART ONLINE

This book is not going to go into detail about how to market online, as it takes an entire book. See *Internet 101* (www.artmarketing.com) and other books.

Using your web site as a portfolio—exhibiting samples of your artwork online—is one effective way to promote your artwork. You want your web site to include everything that a hand-held portfolio contains: bio, statement, pictures of your art, contact info, copies of press clippings or articles about your art, price list as well as a guest book and an interesting story that makes you unique.

ONLINE POSSIBILITIES

- Your own URL, perhaps with a link to Twitter
- Blogging (Google online to find out info: www.howtoblog.org)
- Being part of a larger gallery exhibition

BIGGEST MISTAKES IN ARTISTS' WEB SITES

- No place to capture visitors' e-mail address for future marketing
- Contact info not easily accessible on your web pages
- Site is too flashy and time-consuming
- No prices are listed
- Too many banners and unnecessary ads

TWO ONLINE GUIDES FOR BUILDING WEB SITES

www.webmonkey.com

www.allwebcodesign.com

INSPIRING SITES

www.calatrava.com

www.diegorivera.com

www.ludwigdesign.com

www.designwithnatureltd.com

www.elizabethturnbull.com.au

www.renegriffith.com

WEB SITE INNOVATION

You want to create a connection with potential clients on your web site. Here's how two artists have done that.

★ One artist (www.douglass-truth.com) created a great web site with "Dorothy's Page." Dorothy is a fictional twin sister who confiscates this artist's work and sells it behind his back at a lower price. This idea got me to bookmark his site and go back there periodically to check on possible sale items.

★ Another artist had such an intriguing life story that I couldn't stop reading it and remember her to this day.

ONLINE MARKETING TACTICS

- ★ Create a book list at www.amazon.com related to your expertise in art.
- ★ List your events on other sites that have calendars and event listings: your local art organization, Craigslist, Laughingsquid, Artline, Flavorpill.
- ★ Check out Google's pay-per-click.
- ★ Post something on your home page to entice visitors to come back: Planning to interview a famous artist soon? Planning to write about a particular topic next quarter?
- ★ Offer an online gift certificate, which your patrons can purchase for a friend (see page 52).
- ★ Write an article that will attract art collectors to your site. Get various sites—Artaffairs, Absolutearts, Newsletteraccess, Ezinearticles.com, Helium.com—to carry these articles. Titles could be: Seven Steps to Enjoying Your Purchased Artwork, Suggestions for Displaying Your Artwork, Developing a Sculpture Garden, Caring for your Art Investment.
- ★ Post your press releases on your site for all your visitors to browse: "Artist Sculpts Portraits from Ice," "Artist Helps Raise $20,000 for Animal Shelter," "New York Times Raves about Artist."

❧

This was excerpted from *INTERNET 101 FOR FINE ARTISTS* by Constance Smith, available at www.artmarketing.com

RECOMMENDED READING

Creating Web Pages for Dummies by Bud E Smith

Effective Websites for Artists and Art Groups by Bob Nicholson

I'm on LinkedIn, Now What? by Jason Alba

Internet 101 for Fine Artists by Constance Smith

Chapter 3

Entering the Art Market

Setting the stage

Target market

Competitors

The art of the telephone

10 ways to expand your clientele

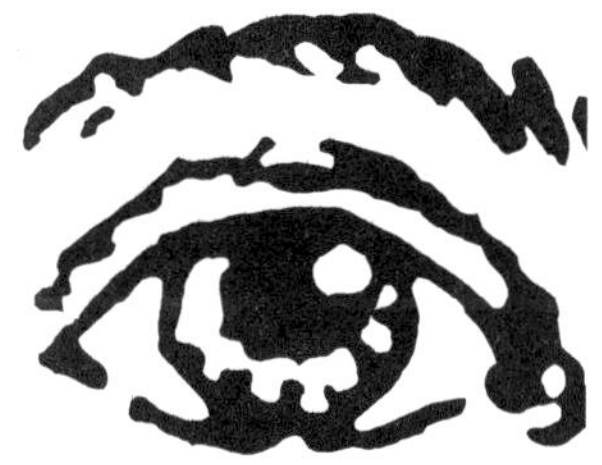

I owe all of my success in life to having always been a quarter of an hour beforehand. Horatio Nelson

SETTING THE STAGE

Great marketers always make some mistakes because they are willing to experiment.

Planning your initial marketing efforts takes time, focus, commitment and knowledge. You need to know as much about the art world as you possibly can. To introduce yourself to potential collectors, you must learn to "swim the waters." All kinds of information about galleries, publishers, shows and competitions will be useful in the progress of your career.

SUPPORT SYSTEM

Setting the stage for an emerging artist means attending art events and openings where you meet other artists, art patrons and the art press. Joining museums or art organizations can help you start to cultivate a support system that will help you attain your goals.

It's important to keep a notebook and files on marketing ideas, strategies, and goals. Look at it periodically to see if you have been attempting to put any of the ideas into action.

Few people are born with business knowledge. People good at business have studied, read magazines in their field, attended seminars, workshops and trade shows. They belong to associations and continue to discover new methods to approach their particular market. Learning about marketing is an ongoing process. Make this quest for new marketing knowledge part of your monthly business activities. With practice, you'll become a confident marketer.

You need to know what is special about your work. If you don't know, you won't be able to tell anyone.

GETTING READY

Your artwork must be ready for the marketplace. If you cannot answer yes to the following questions, you are not quite ready to begin your career.

- Are you able to produce artwork of a consistent quality and style?
- Is the quality of your work up to the standards of the market?
- Do you have a body of work ready (20 pieces) to sell?
- Is your "voice" recognizable? (See page 15.)
- Are you able to produce enough pieces per month to keep up with future demand?
- Do you have legal considerations, such as model releases, in order?
- Are you psychologically ready for the possible onslaught of criticism?
- Are you willing to part with your artwork?
- Do you consider the prices you've calculated to be agreeable to you?

TARGET MARKET

As you start researching places to sell your work, remember that your main goal is to get your work in front of the public for reviewing. If they don't see it, they can't react, nor can they buy. Your first aim should not be a New York gallery—or any gallery, for that matter. If that's your aim, you're hoeing a difficult path. (Make a gallery your priority only after you have gained a reputation.)

A target market is the group of people toward whom you will concentrate your sales efforts. Many artists overlook sales opportunities that could be quite profitable to them and think only of getting into a gallery. Artists I am acquainted with who are making a living from the sale of their artwork earn most of their income from sources other than galleries.

Niche market

Take a notebook and answer the questions below. You will then have a better understanding of the specific people who might like to purchase your artwork, where to find them, and how to attract them. This is your niche market. Don't be misled to think that the larger the niche market, the more sales you will have. Small is good: Word spreads fast in a small group.

WHO IS ATTRACTED TO MY ARTWORK?

❑ Men ❑ Women ❑ Children

❑ All ____________

Marital status ____________

Ethnic background ____________

Age group ____________

Religion ____________

Income level ____________

Education level ____________

What do they read? ____________

Where do they hang out? ____________

How can I get their attention? ____________

What are their reasons for buying my art? ____________

What organizations do they belong to? ____________

Specific region of the country to sell to? ____________

Describe exactly what I am selling. ____________

Define more specifically my target market. ____________

Features of my artwork. ____________

Benefits to buyer: Can I offer something more, something different, something better than my competitors? ____________

Experience, authority, expertise: Why would someone trust me? ____________

How will buying my artwork make the customer's life better? ____________

How can people pay for their purchase (credit card, check, terms)? Will this satisfy my target market?

Am I able to produce enough original pieces for potential buyers in my target market? ____________

Are there any legal considerations in selling my product to this (or any other) market? ____________

COMPETITORS

Check out your competition

The reason you study the competition is to learn how and why they are successful. Believe me, there is enough room for all of you. An artist I spoke to recently on the telephone told me how inspired he had become when viewing the California Watercolor Society Show held in downtown San Francisco. Being a watercolorist himself, he had found it "totally awe-inspiring" to see what his fellow artists—competitors—were accomplishing.

I think artists avoid looking at their fellow artists' work, either from fear of imitating or from feeling demeaned by the power of their "competitors'" work. A new attitude needs to be induced in order to survive in this day and age—an attitude of sharing.

Some artists regard joining an art organization with this same type of reaction—a fear of competition. They become intimidated when meeting other artists who are creating and marketing their artwork successfully, once again thinking of them as competition. Start thinking of competitors as colleagues. Then you will start to become an empowered group instead of a group that is separated by competitiveness.

A short quiz

Who is your competition and why (style, quality, technique, price)?

Locally ____

Regionally ____

Nationally ____

Who are the large, known players in the niche you are after?

Do you have an advantage that allows you to carve out a position?

Do you have referrals to this niche?

How are you different from others? Be specific.

What do they do better than you?

What do you do better than them?

Have you seen any of their literature or web sites?

What ideas can you "borrow" from them?

Where do they market that you don't?

Do they offer more services than you do?

Are your prices similar?

The Art of the Telephone

In this day and age, the telephone is still an important tool. Many artists have difficulty using the telephone to call a stranger; even well-versed salesmen start out with this problem. The way to overcome this fear is by practicing. The telephone is one of the handiest tools in an office. Though e-mail is a great tool for connecting, the voice is still a major tool for an "intimate" business connection, and that's what you need when you make an art-related sale.

Using the telephone is a learned art. Download "Client Status Record" to help you with the process at www.artmarketing.com/downloads.html.

You must attempt to develop a positive attitude toward using this great tool. Once you get used to talking on the phone, it will become second nature. Don't expect to be an expert in one month. You will improve each time you talk.

- Don't think you have to sell art over the phone. With a phone call, you are generally informing a person of your whereabouts, the possibility of viewing your work, or perhaps asking for an appointment or studio visit.
- Know what you want to accomplish before you call. Write it down in a brief outline—a script.
- Make calls in groups of the same type: follow-up, sales, friendly reminder. You will pick up momentum psychologically and it will become easier.
- Pick the correct time to call; you will not always know, but do your best. Right before lunch or office closing time is not so good. If you think there is an emergency that might arise in your personal life during the moments you plan a call, or if you are expecting a call from someone, postpone your call.

Etiquette

- When you get hold of the person you desire to speak with, ask if he has a moment. This shows respect, and he will honor that. If he is in the middle of something, volunteer to call at a more convenient time.
- Don't interrupt a call you've started by taking an incoming call. Your client will find this rude. You need to have your phone system set up with call messaging so you can talk while a message is being taken.

Getting Past a Receptionist

One of the main responsibilities of a receptionist is to screen calls. Some executives even give their receptionist the power to decide which calls to refer to them and which to fend off. Show the receptionist respect—the same respect that you would show her boss. Your aim should be to become friends with her. She can be key in introducing you to her boss. If she likes you, you may come highly recommended!

Chapter 9 of *Selling Art 101* provides a wonderful education on closing a sale and more.

One of the most common mistakes in business is not realizing the importance of a follow-up call. To make a sale or get an editor interested in coming to an opening usually takes repeated, follow-up contact.

Client status record

As you begin to make more phone calls and to contact art professionals, it will become increasingly difficult to remember what you said to whom. Start using a "Client Status Record" (download a copy at www.artmarketing.com/downloads.html) for each new client. When someone contacts you, pull out your notebook to refresh your memory on her history.

The first call

When you make a first call, it is an introduction, perhaps to verify an address or see if the person is interested in viewing your work. Try to gauge by the tone of voice how interested the person is. (Add any pertinent information to your Client Status Record for future reference.) If the person is not interested but is friendly, ask "Could you recommend a more appropriate gallery (consultant, publisher)?"

First follow-up call

After an interested person has reviewed your work, you will need to make a follow-up call. Be mentally focused when you make this call. Beforehand, brief yourself on different possibilities of what the conversation might lead to. (Don't spend too much time on this prepping or you'll get nervous.) The first few times you do this type of follow-up call, you will make errors, get nervous, but after several times you'll have it down.

Make a follow-up call about five days after you think a person has reviewed your work. E-mails do not suffice for follow-up. Reach them on the telephone, introduce yourself and ask if they've had a chance to review your work. Perhaps they've been busy, out of town, at meetings for two weeks. If they haven't reviewed your portfolio or web site, ask them if you can call them back in three days or so. This gives them a timeframe to review your work. Mark it on your calendar and call back in three days. No later. No sooner.

Second follow-up call

Here is where most people err. They do not make the second follow-up call. In three days, when you call back and get their answering machine, leave a brief message, but say you will call back in a couple of days. This could go on for some time. Keep trying every few days. At some point, if they don't return your call, you can act a little more aggressive—but not nasty—when you leave a message.

Sometimes their call will precede yours. This is an excellent sign, but don't show too much excitement or enthusiasm. Don't think this means, "Yes, I want to exhibit your work in my gallery." This is only one step in the process of building a business relationship. Take one step at a time.

One way to conquer a fear is to attack it. Attack the phone fear by spending more time on the phone.

Calling tips

- Set up a schedule for making calls—at the same hour of the same day each week. This will help you get in a routine. Routine is often what you need in order to do something you don't like to do. Set a goal as to how many prospects you will call during this time—say, five to 10 calls each time. Reward yourself after the session by doing something you like.
- Try warming up your telephone voice by calling a couple of friends or relatives first.
- Introduce yourself to the person you call, and make it clear who you are, where you met or who referred you.
- Put notes on important facts and issues you discuss onto your Client Status Record. This is called "smart calling." You will impress your client with what you've remembered next time you speak.
- Call from a quiet place free of interruptions.
- Rehearse your presentation and anticipate people's responses.
- Know your topic and have all the facts at hand.
- Be psychologically prepared and centered. Prepare a checklist of points to follow.
- Know who you are calling and why. This is not a cold call; you have done your research.
- Don't justify your work, or anything else for that matter.
- Know the benefits for this person of doing business with you. Make a list of them before you dial.
- Have your calendar handy for preparing a meeting date or studio visit.
- Speak clearly and concisely.
- Be positive; be prepared for objections.
- Always thank the listener for his time.
- When you call, don't waste people's time. Let the customer lead. Does he want to chat? Is he in a hurry?

Answer the phone slowly with your company name (or personal name). When I call a big business, it often happens that I cannot understand the person answering the phone because they are talking so fast. This is sloppy as well as frustrating. If you have an employee, make sure she is answering the phone pleasantly, slowly and clearly.

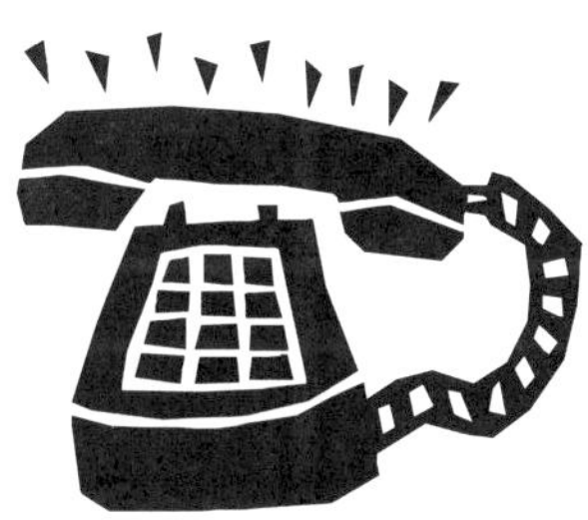

Practice makes perfect.

MAKING SALES CALLS

by Robert Regis Dvorák

The best time to make a sales call is mid-morning after 10:00. People generally feel fresher and more receptive after they've had their coffee or tea. After lunch, a lot of people feel sluggish. Near the end of the day, many people get tired and are less receptive.

Be perceptive and listen to the tone of the other person's voice. If she sounds like she is busy and really doesn't want to talk to you right then, ask when a good time to call back would be. Suggest *two* times. This consideration will be appreciated. When you call back, the person will be more inclined to talk to you.

Salesperson: "It sounds like you are in the middle of something, Bill. I can call you back later this afternoon or the first thing in the morning. Which would be better for you?"

Script important calls

It is helpful to script your important telephone calls. Write out what you are going to say and the anticipated answers. Try to think of all the possible responses and script out your follow-up statements. Practice your script with a friend on the phone before making the call. This will give you the confidence you need when you make the actual call.

Exercise

Write a script for a call you want to make but have been procrastinating over because you don't want to be turned down or embarrassed. Practice the script with a friend a number of times. Make adjustments to your script, then make the call and write the result on your Client Status Record.

Warm calls

The easiest calls to make are what I call warm calls. These are calls that follow up a chance meeting you had, a referral, or an inquiry on your answering machine. These kinds of calls give you a better chance for getting an appointment.

- ★ Be flexible. Go to them if they can't or don't seem willing to come visit you.
- ★ Be prepared to handle objections to setting up a meeting.
- ★ Be sure that when you schedule a meeting, the decision-maker will be present.
- ★ If it is a couple, be sure that both parties will be present at any visit.
- ★ Answer questions and then ask a question.
- ★ Use questions to move the call along quickly to an appointment. Your client will appreciate your efficiency.

❧

The above is an excerpt from Chapter 6 of *SELLING ART 101, 2ND EDITION*. You can read more about this book online at www.artmarketing.com/books.

10 Ways to Expand Your Clientele

Try to see the world from your customer's point of view.

Know your niche

The niche you choose is a natural offshoot of your style. One artist I know does houses—"Soul Paintings" of people's abodes, both interior and exterior. They are wonderful and interesting. Even when it is someone else's home, people are attracted to the painting. Another artist paints close-up shots, mostly portraits of dogs in vibrant colors. Find a niche.

Do your homework

Research your market. How can you personally reach the clientele for your niche? Become familiar with magazines your niche audience reads. For promotional purposes, try to have your artwork reproduced on the cover of one of these magazines.

Keep your business personal

As an artist, you are running a personal service company. You need to be accommodating. If you are personable in a natural way, this will get you far. By trying to understand how you can help a potential customer, you will gain clients of long-lasting duration as well as ones who refer you to new clients.

Keep it legal

Be sure to get a model release from any person (even a relative) before you execute a painting. Even if it is a portrait commission, you will want a model release; then you will have the rights for reproduction and exhibition. You will need to get a model release for buildings you paint (from the owner of the building) if you plan to sell or reproduce the artwork.

Take a few small risks

Every business owner must take risks to advance. Invest $250 for a booth at an art fair. Learn from failures, switch gears and keep growing.

Be persistent

Keep putting your work in front of potential customers who fit your niche market. Make it your goal to talk to one new person each week who can assist you on your career path.

Presentation

Present your artwork and self professionally. This could mean the addition of a simple frame, a printed sign instead of a handwritten one, or a thank-you note. Be sure to put your URL on everything you hand out and anything you sell, such as a business card on the back of your painting.

If you ever get a referral, be sure you thank by card or phone the person who gave it to you, even if you don't make a final sale. You want to have any excuse you can to call someone who was nice enough to give you a referral. That way he'll give you another.

Start small

Don't expect overnight success, but do expect results. If your results are consistent, they tend *not* to fall off quickly. Aim up the slow road and stay on it. Aim for making 25% on your investment. There's no sense in giving away all your work at a super low price, but if you can keep below the general market by a few bucks, you'll make more sales.

Get ink

Keep the press informed. Develop story lines to keep your local art, home or horticulture editor informed of your developments. This pays off in the long run—people start talking, and that's the best advertising. Choose your publications carefully. Know their audience and reason for existence. Study back issues of publications to determine the slant, thus enabling you to understand how your subject matter can best benefit the readers.

- Be aware of deadlines: daily, weekly and monthly.
- Be innovative: Help your editors by suggesting story lines to them.
- Give an exclusive: Tell an editor with whom you have a special relationship that you will give her an exclusive on a story line.
- Be courteous to your editors. When they are on deadline, they can be very stressed. Before you start "chatting" with an editor, make sure she is not on deadline.

Accept credit cards

It is imperative in this day and age for you to be able to accept credit cards. You will miss sales opportunities if you don't. Online sources such as PayPal provide this possibility without much hassle. The 3% service fee is well worth the deductible expense.

- Spur-of-the-moment buying is prompted.
- Convenient for telephone orders
- Security: Peace of mind for your customers could be a guarantee.
- Quick deposit. A bank generally applies a credit card charge within three days to your account, whereas it might hold an out-of-state check for a week or more.

Chapter 4

Sales Techniques

Learning to sell

Handling objections

Follow-up

A science to purchasing

Leasing art

Patron programs

Gift certificates

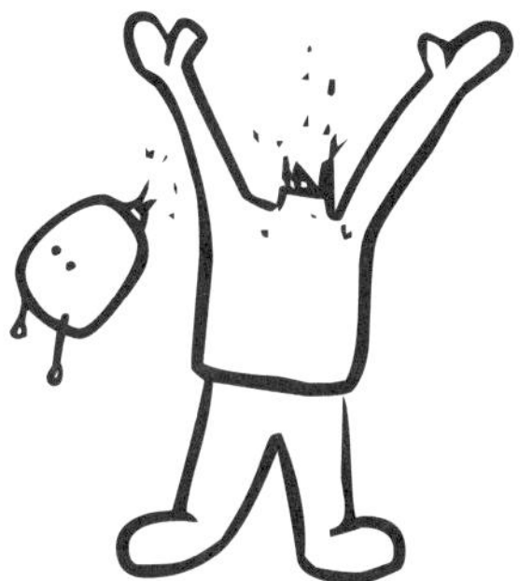

Search others for their virtues.
Benjamin Franklin

LEARNING TO SELL

Art mostly sells itself.

Most people will say that it's hard to sell art, that no one wants to buy art. They are wrong. There are plenty of people who want to buy art, want to improve their lifestyle, want to feel good about themselves, enjoy art.

Art has been made out to be a thing for the rich. How absurd! I've bought many original works of art for under $250. At outdoor art fairs and co-op galleries there are beautiful pieces ranging from $50 and up.

The term "marketing" is sometimes used incorrectly as a synonym for selling.

- Marketing is the sum of several different kinds of activities: promotion, intelligent research, planning, pricing, studying competition.
- Selling is the act of getting money in exchange for a product—in this case, your artwork.

"Sales" usually implies luring people into a trap and selling them something they don't want. This is not the approach you want to take as an artist. It will surely backfire.

EXCUSES YOU MAKE

Everyone who comes before you is a potential client. If you have excuses for why not to sell to someone, it is most likely because you don't want to make the effort. When you are in a confident mood, you will not have excuses. Practice not having these common excuses:

- He doesn't look like someone who buys art.
- She is not avant-garde enough for my art.
- Her fingernails are not polished. She doesn't have any money.
- No one off a tour bus ever buys.

The easiest place to sell your art is from your studio. People ask me all the time, "Where is the most active art market in the U.S.?" When I tell them it's their own studio, they get really mad. They want to hear some magical answer like Santa Fe, New York, Seattle.

STUDYING OTHER ARTISTS' SALES TECHNIQUES

Keep in mind as you read this chapter what type of salespeople you would like to emulate. When you go to galleries, study how they do it. When you visit an outdoor art fair or an exhibit at a local art center, see how they do it. You will want to observe all types of salespeople and see how you react to them. Write your comments down. Learning your own buying style will teach you your best selling style. You will find some common denominators in the people you can deal with comfortably:

- You trust them; somehow they have gained your confidence.
- You like them; you might even consider them as future friends.

I was a juror on a court case. The prosecutor was a mild-mannered lawyer—you could barely hear his voice. The defense attorney was a power-infested madman. No one on the jury liked the defense attorney, although he appeared more like a winning lawyer. None of us wanted to listen to this disgusting defense attorney. I believe he lost his case mostly because people didn't like his personality. Likewise, if you sound like a stereotypical car salesman, people will walk away from you in an instant. Be natural, honest and kind, and you will sell more art. Pretend you are talking to someone in your own home about your artwork when you speak with a potential buyer.

You are giving people an opportunity when they buy your artwork—an opportunity to add a new dimension to their life.

HANDLING OBJECTIONS

Listen to your clients. Chat with them at your openings. Find out what they like or want—perhaps a new size of painting, a new medium (giclée), help with hanging their artwork. Personalize, personalize, personalize.

Unless someone is ready to make a purchase, she generally will have objections to handing over cash. As you proceed with your sales, you will become more familiar with what is a normal objection and what is a difficult objection. One way to get around objections is by changing the subject and simply not answering them, or by asking another question.

- **Some people might not be sure if they actually like the piece**. They need reaffirmation—from a bystander, their mate, a friend. In this case, you could offer them a money-back guarantee. They can display it for two weeks in their home. Then they'll have a chance to hear comments from friends and neighbors.
- **The price is out of their budget.** Your answer would be, "How about a lease?" or "Why don't you join my Patron Program (see page 50) and pay by the month?" or "I do have a layaway plan." If you accept credit cards, you might feel secure with giving them the piece with three installments on a credit card.
- **Price is too high.** They are not familiar with the serigraph process and think it is a poster. Educate them. Suggest they compare your prices to the artist down the street, or tell them that you just sold a piece to so-and-so or that your prices have risen slowly over the years because you are more in demand.
- **The colors clash with their room.** Show them a different but similar piece. Teach them that an art piece is what sets off a room, not the couch.
- **They don't feel they deserve such a fine piece.** This might not be said in words, but it is how some people have been trained to feel, especially new collectors who haven't had time to begin to appreciate art in their homes. Explain that everyone deserves to have a living image to view daily.
- **"I can't make up my mind."** Make them feel confident in their choice. You could introduce them to the Patron Program (see page 50) so they have more time and more choice.
- **Silent objection.** They won't look you in the eye, they have nervous energy, their arms are folded, they won't shake your hand. Make them feel confident in you. Show them your portfolio, listing what museums your work is in.

SOLVE YOUR CUSTOMER'S PROBLEM

Think of selling as solving a potential client's problem. Some of them have an easier time letting themselves be rewarded with artwork. For others, it is new territory and they don't feel confident. For still others, someone else has imposed the problem; they have reached a certain financial status and others expect them to be owners of original artwork. They really don't know what they like, what they want. They want to be told and want to trust the person telling them.

Never ask a question of a potential client that can be answered with a simple "Yes" or "No."

Instill confidence

You need to instill confidence in buyers. Knowing detailed information about an artist or his creative process can help a potential buyer become more confident. A buyer has to respond to the work.

- If you sell at the same outdoor art fair for several years running, this fosters confidence. You are not an art peddler; you are an art dealer, which requires a relationship on an ongoing basis.
- Being referred by a friend or associate is a confidence-builder.
- Someone they know owns your work and loves it.
- The local arts council or museum has a piece of your work.
- They saw your name in an article in the local paper.

Listen

When you listen and feed back to a child what he is saying, it instills trust and confidence. The same is true in sales. If your customer has a need and you listen, perhaps you can fulfill it and make a sale.

Learn to chat with people. If they say something interesting on the phone, such as where they are calling from or what they did on the weekend, ask them something more. People love that intimacy.

Sell benefits

People want to be sold benefits. Buyers want to know the benefits of owning *your* artwork. So, make a list of these benefits right now! A benefit generally saves time, energy or money while appealing to the ego. Right color, right size, joyous feeling, the artist is collected by a loyal following, critics say good things about the artist, nicely framed high-quality materials. All can be benefits of owning a piece of art.

Benefits of owning my art

____

____

____

____

____

____

SUCCESSFUL SELLING

by Renée Phillips

Stress the benefits

The selling of art begins with an awareness and expression of its benefits. Rejoice in the fact that art has communicative and healing powers; it enriches owners' lives. It has the power to educate and can alter viewers' attitudes and behaviors. When someone buys your work, a permanent bond is formed. You should thoroughly savor the joyful process of sharing and exchanging it for money and recognition.

Set financial goals

Success and prosperity are subjective terms. You will attract that which you desire—however small or grand. Set a financial goal and a deadline. Commit yourself to the same high standards for your financial rewards as you do for your art. If you are frustrated with your current financial situation—good! Channel the anger into a determined effort to change. Define your sales objectives and seek professional feedback about your work and its relationship to the art market. Create a balanced, diversified plan for your unpredictable career course. Review it regularly, be flexible, and alter it when necessary. To insure your success, include plans to share your prosperity generously with others, beginning now.

❧

Renée Phillips is a promotion and marketing consultant for artists, available for private consultation in person or by phone. She can be contacted at www.manhattanarts.com.

FOUR SALES MISTAKES

- Trying to sell to someone who just wants to talk
- Lying or insincerity
- Talking too much
- Forgetting to build a relationship

There is no way around investing time and energy in your clients.

FOLLOW-UP

One of the major pitfalls in business is not following up on leads.

Follow up a short time after a sale is made with a friendly call to your client. Yes! He's *your* client now. He's moved up the ladder to #1 code on your mailing list. Call to see if all is going well with his purchase. Tell him briefly about your new paintings. Ask him if he needs any more work for his office or if he has a friend who's been looking for art. Perhaps it's a little hard at first to be forward like this. Keep it friendly. Try it! He likes you. He likes your work. He bought from you. He's happy. Now you are connecting again so he won't forget you.

- After you make this call, send the client (whether he has given you a referral or not) a brief note, 3-5 business cards, a flier/postcard/color photocopy of your newest piece and perhaps a discount coupon (see page 52) toward his next purchase.
- If the sale has been made to a business, you might stop in to see "how my baby's doing." You might meet some employees and leave your business card on the front desk with the receptionist. Casually—no pressure. Send annual cards to the buyer and perhaps one to the office staff.

Referrals

Don't forget to ask for a referral. Many art world professionals are glad to refer you to someone they know. Private buyers love to help an artist in her career efforts.

When you do receive a referral, be sure to follow through. A referral call is an easy call to make. Someone sent you; that recipient doesn't want to be impolite when a friend has recommended you to him. So when you introduce yourself, be sure to state who sent you. "Hi, Mr. Thomas. My name is . . . and I was referred by Sally Parker of Time Inc to call you about my artwork. She thought you might be interested in reviewing my portfolio for a possible show in your corporate gallery."

Whatever the outcome, make sure you drop a thank-you note to Sally Parker for her referral. Include a couple of your business cards. Only hint for her to pass them out. If you actually make a sale to a referral, write another note of thanks and include a coupon for a discount on one of your paintings: "Thanks again for your assistance in making my career a success. I hung a piece in Mr. Thomas's office yesterday. As a thank-you for your patronage, I would like to offer you a 20% discount on a purchase from my collection. Why don't you come by my studio sometime? I can help you decide what piece might be best in your office. Prints are now available of some of my works (flier enclosed)." Small, personal offerings will help bring successful sales.

Send your new collectors home with an artist pack: a folder with your business card, resume, statement, bio, and photocopied articles. Make them proud.

A SCIENCE TO PURCHASING

Persistence is what makes a good salesperson. An outstanding salesperson contacts a prospect an average of three times, usually within a three-to-six-month period. The outstanding seller makes five to seven contacts each day.

80/20 RULE

Eighty percent of your income comes from 20% of your clients. Think about this and you will know why you want to court the people who have already purchased from you. Treat them specially and they will pass the word along about how great your artwork is.

- Send them a postcard periodically, updating them on your latest piece.
- A little gift goes a long way. One artist made a limited-edition print of a Christmas card and sent it to her special customers.
- Notify previous buyers about articles that have been written about you or a new corporate collection your work is in. If they hear you are prospering, it means their artwork is going up in value. They like that and will want to support you even more.

TWO GREAT BOOKS

Yes! 50 Scientifically Proven Ways to Be Persuasive by Noah Goldstein, Steve J Martin and Robert B Cialdin. Some of the scientific studies show how the human race is gullible: crowd mentality and more. Gather ideas on how to change your sales and marketing tactics. www.influenceatwork.com

Why We Buy: The Science of Shopping by Paco Underhill. A most interesting read. Here are some tips I learned:

- Transitioning from outside to inside a store is a time when people do not "see" things, so placing something in the doorway is not a good sales tactic.
- Most of us are right-handed and turn to the right upon entering a room; thus, you should place your most important painting on the right-hand side inside the entrance.
- Have some seats scattered around your studio where clients can rest while they contemplate your artwork. This sends the message that you care. The comfort zone of seats—cozy ones—allows them to stay a bit longer. The longer shoppers stay in a store, the more likely they will become buyers.
- The sense of touch is important. Have some artwork that a person can lift off a shelf and touch without damaging. It involves them more deeply in the space and creates a sense of reality. Have a sign stating "Please Touch."
- Involving the olfactory nerves helps in creating more sales. Burn aromatic candles to create a subtle fragrance.
- Customers do not like: obscure price tags, intimidating service, having to ask dumb questions, lines, too many mirrors.

LEASING ART

Reduce the risk for your customers by selling them small on your first approach, or have them lease. Get your foot in the door. Get them hooked on your artwork, then sell them an original.

One of the most frequent programs I sold as a rep, especially to businesses, was that of the lease. A lease is not really different from a rental, except that it lasts longer than just a one-month period. Suggesting a lease to clients made it easier for me to get my foot in the door of a small business. It also created a flow of income, both for the artist and for myself as a rep. To my surprise, many individual company employees began to lease for their homes. Incidentally, I never had one piece damaged or stolen.

The consumer enjoys supporting local artists in a way he can afford. He may think he can't afford an original at $3500. A quarterly fee may be within his budget. Lease options work like this:

- The client chooses a piece he wishes to lease for a three-month period, with possible renewal of up to one year (or whatever you decide is reasonable).
- Setup fee $_______.
- The piece is leased according to its selling price, usually at 2% per month of the selling price. (2% x 3 months + setup fee)
- Lease payments can go toward the purchase (not the setup fee). Often, all the lease money paid for the first 12 months is applied toward the purchase price.
- Make sure you have an agreement signed by both parties. Download a Lease Agreement at www.artmarketing.com/downloads.html.
- The company will be liable for damage or theft, to the full price of the piece.
- Provide a standard "Care of Artwork" sheet (download a copy at www.artmarketing.com/downloads.html).
- Guard against risk if they claim bankruptcy by noting that your artwork is not owned by the business, only leased.

PATRON PROGRAMS

In the Renaissance era, having a patron was not unusual for an artist. In our time, artists often neglect to consider this method of support.

Find a person who likes your artwork. Ask if he would like to participate in your career by making a $100 per-month commitment toward a new piece of artwork. He continues to pay $100 per month until he can afford a piece of your work. During that time, he can visit your studio, and if he sees any work-in-progress he would like to purchase, he can claim it as his future piece. When his monthly payments equal the piece's price, he can take the piece home. He also has the option of speeding up payments to pay for the piece on the spot. Draw up a user-friendly contract to clarify all the details of your patronage program. (*Art Office,* published by ArtNetwork, includes many legal agreements for artists. Available at www.artmarketing.com.)

GENERATE BUZZ ON A SHOESTRING

She wanted to go to China. It was a cultural tour and the chance of a lifetime, but the ticket alone was $3200. How would she pay for it without going into debt? Karen Bubb, a mixed-media artist and public arts manager for the Boise, Idaho City Arts Commission, is also a big fan of solving problems with the help of artist-friends. And it's a good thing she values the input of others. One trusted advisor gave Karen the suggestion that helped her get to China. The advisor recommended that Karen sell "shares" of the experience. If she could sell 100 "shares" at $32 each, Karen could pay for her trip. That's all well and good, but even someone as well connected to her community as Karen had to ask why people would buy shares of a trip to China that they would never take.

She would have to give the shares value. The package she eventually came up with enticed potential shareholders with enormous value for only $32 a share!

In return for $32, here is what Karen promised her "shareholders."

- A "stock certificate:" a hand-pulled print created by Karen that doubled as a thank-you note for their purchase.
- A handmade collaged postcard sent from China
- A small (6x5 1/2") encaustic painting based on the trip and Karen's experience in China
- An invitation to attend a private party and slide show after the trip

Karen committed to the trip in January 2004 and was due to leave on May 26. A reporter got wind of her plan, and an article appeared in the April 17 issue of the Boise newspaper. Her plan to sell shares to family, friends, and colleagues exploded to include anyone who wanted to participate. Before she knew it, Karen had sold 225 shares, 30% of which went to total strangers who wanted to be part of the experience.

And she had just over a month to make everything come together.

What started as an adventure to a distant land became something bigger because of the way Karen promoted herself. Her trip was now a performance piece. The connections to her shareholders were powerful and informed every decision. She spent much of the month prior to her departure making the collaged postcards that would be sent from China, as promised, to each shareholder. She used the additional funds to purchase an audio recorder and camera to document the trip accurately and artistically.

Upon her return from China, Karen worked for two and one-half years to produce the promised paintings to her shareholders. When they were completed, the paintings were exhibited as a group before being dispersed. The gallery that had long represented Karen was supportive of her decisions and funding methods. The open dialogue between artist and gallery eased minds and assured both parties that it was a win win situation. It also lessened the risk of any surprises in the professional relationship.

Karen says she'd do it all over again and probably pay closer attention to creating a realistic budget. When asked if, given the large amount of work she needed to produce following the trip, she might charge more for shareholders, Karen hesitated and said it wouldn't be above $50 per share. Part of the success and the fun was involving so many people in the process. She clarified:

"I gained numerous fans by just completing it and doing what I said I was going to do. I probably lost money in the end in that I did not factor in all of the costs of doing the body of work in terms of material and time, but I gained an incredible relationship with many collectors and community members. I also did a body of work I wouldn't have done otherwise, which was very satisfying indeed."

❧

Excerpted from *I'd Rather Be in the Studio! The Artist's No-Excuse Guide to Self-Promotion* by Alyson Stanfield. Alyson shows artists how to promote their art more effectively through her book, newsletter, and the resources at www.ArtBizCoach.com and www.ArtBizBlog.com.

Guarantee

Let your potential customers know that your work is guaranteed: If the client is not happy with his piece, he can return it. If this happens, ask him if he'd like to try a different piece. Most likely he doesn't have quite enough confidence yet. You will be able to help instill confidence in his decision if you can see the environment where his work is to be installed and suggest an appropriate piece. Perhaps there is an outside objection: His wife was surprised that he spent $2000 on a painting when she would rather have purchased a wardrobe. In this case, you would have to impress the wife.

GIFT CERTIFICATES

Make sure appropriate contact information is on the certificate so it's easy to contact you.

Promoting the purchase of gift certificates can bring more sales than you might expect. Use the pre-formatted gift certificate forms that your local office supply store sells and add details on your home printer. Keep a log of whom you sell a certificate to and an ID# to match the certificate. When you fulfill a certificate, be sure to add that person to your mailing list.

- Promote the purchase of gift certificates around the holidays.
- Have gift certificates ready for purchase at your next studio show: "This gift certificate is a gift from ________________." Put a dollar amount on it.
- Do not charge a fee to the purchaser of the gift—only the certificate amount.
- When someone makes a purchase, award her with a 20% discount coupon towards her next purchase. Make sure she understands what a great deal this is. It's a good deal for you too: Obtaining a new client costs five times as much as getting an established one to repurchase.
- Send prevous clients a discount coupon when you send them a postcard to your next show.
- Create a coupon-postcard for your next studio show or art opening

This entitles John Smith to a
discount of 20%
off his next purchase.

#77

Frank Salisbury, marine artist www.marineartist.com 520.671.3423
One coupon per artwork.

GIFT CERTIFICATE

To ________________________

A certificate worth **$75** has been given you by ________________________

towards the purchase of an artwork from Frank Salisbury, marine artist.

Set up a time to visit and browse at

www.marineartist.com or call 520.671.3423.

#GC12

Attracting and Keeping Clients

by Robert Regis Dvorák

As a salesperson, have your objective be not only to make sales but also to meet and keep clients. Remember, your clients should be for a lifetime. Each individual you meet is important and deserving of your highest regard. Treat everyone with dignity.

Telling is not selling

One of the most effective ways to complete a sale is to engage in a dialogue with the potential client in which you ask questions that will lead to a buying decision. Salespersons not trained in selling art usually try to tell their clients about the works they represent. My experience has taught me that clients might politely listen for a minute or so, but as the representative continues to talk, they become less and less interested. By telling, you will end up losing their attention and a sale. People don't like to be told. They would rather tell you! The way to get your clients really interested in owning what you have to sell them—art—is to ask them questions so that they can tell you their thoughts. The more they tell you, the more interested they will become.

Giving more than is expected

To be successful in the business of selling art, think of ways to develop a loyal clientele—collectors who will buy from you again and again. One way to do that is to give your clients more than they expect. It could be a poster, a large postcard featuring one of your works, an invitation to a private showing, a print, a small sketch, a book that features your works. You have all sorts of things around your studio that you could make into a thank-you gift for your clients—something that your clients will appreciate. Gone are the days when you make a sale and the next day forget to whom you sold. Your best clients will become good friends and loyal collectors. Your best clients will also become your best publicity agents for finding new clients to increase your sales.

Tone of voice

Your tone of voice has a profound influence on the mood and rapport that you will have with your clients. Ask your good friends to comment on your tone of voice. Do you speak too loudly or too softly? Does your voice sound harsh? Do you speak too fast or too slowly?

Learn to be aware of your tone of voice. Find out if it has the effect of making people feel relaxed. One way to become more aware of this is to set up a tape recorder and record conversations with a friend. Play it back; listen to your voice.

❧

This article was excerpted from Chapter 3 of *Selling Art 101* by Robert Regis Dvorák, available at www.artmarketing.com.

Chapter 5

Promotional Pieces

Direct mail

Competent design

Postcards

Mailing lists

E- newsletters

Criticism is easy, art is difficult.
Destauches

DIRECT MAIL

Direct mail is the process of sending a mailer—postcard, brochure, flyer—through the postal system.

Keeping in contact with current as well as potential clients is an important part of marketing. Direct mail should be part of any promotional campaign. Promotion needs to occur in a variety of ways: through trade shows, art fairs, exhibitions, web sites, personal contact, press. With careful planning, the cost of a direct mail promotion can be covered by the sales it ultimately brings.

For your own in-house mailing list—the list you created through research, web site visits and purchasers—it's a great way to invite clients to a show, your biannual open studio, or private visits to your studio to see your newest work.

SUCCESSFUL MAILERS

- Have great copy; can be read easily
- Arouse curiosity
- Have a great offer
- Use a strong mailing list: quality not quantity. Choosing to mail to 50-100 hand-picked clients can be one of your best choices.
- Sell benefits, not features, with the best benefit in the headline copy
- Tell recipients exactly what you want them to do: "Buy my newest piece—only $1500."
- Don't forget URL, telephone, e-mail, location and time of exhibit
- Adhere to postal guidelines: Square postcards cost over 10¢ more per piece, yet may be worth using as they stand out more.
- Make the recipient feel needed and welcome: "I can't wait to see you at my reception" hand-written on the mailer.

Keep track of each mailing and the responses. Did potential clients use the discount coupon? Plan a long term campaign: three mailings to 50 people within the year.

TRY

- Adding a fragrance to the mailer
- Having a free gift awaiting recipients when they come to your Open Studio
- Varying the size of the mailer
- Noting "Bring a friend" on an invitation
- Creating a postcard that is a discount coupon
- Getting your client to visit your web site by having something special to see: a video of you working, a tour of your studio, your new work

Decide

- What you should mail: postcard, brochure, flyer
- When you should mail
- To whom you should mail

Ask yourself

- What is the purpose of this promo piece?
- What is my budget?
- Who am I trying to reach?
- What is a design style that could pleasantly surprise? How am I different? Why should a person respond to my mailer? Which writing style would he understand?
- What kind of image do I want to create?
- What's a special benefit that could "catch" my audience?
- What is the type of testimonial that would appeal?

Three times a charm

I'm sure you've heard of this saying in real life, but it also applies to business—three times a charm. Mailing to the same group of people consistently will give you more responses to each additional mailing. In the art world, this is especially true: Gallery owners want to know an artist is doing business for more than one exhibit. Once they see you have open studios, are showing and selling at your local art center, they will want to investigate you. Success breeds success.

The three-time effect is also true when introducing a new idea to someone (even your partner or child).

- The first attempt is to introduce a new idea. The reply may be an instant "No."
- Give them some time to think about your idea before you drop the second hint. The reply may still be a strong "No," but not such a harsh one. You can tell they've considered the idea.
- If your timing is right and you bring up the subject again, the third attempt might receive a "Yes." If not, you might, at least, be able to have a discussion about the topic. Progress comes with patience.

When you mail a promotional piece that is a bit different, professionals tend to keep it longer—maybe even post it on their bulletin boards. And that's the idea—to get them to keep it and eventually call you or attend an event.

COMPETENT DESIGN

Save mailings you receive that you particularly like. By studying these, you will get a feeling for the type of mailer you might want to create.

Unless you are a gifted graphic designer, hire a professional to design your mailer. Unprofessional graphic design just doesn't cut it in today's marketplace.

Have the basic ideas you want to express and the basic style you like, then present those to a graphic designer who can put it together with a winning design. Use some of the elements you already have pulled together: your logo, your web site design, previous mailers.

Good design in direct mail includes complying with Post Office regulations. With any unusual design, we recommend asking your local Post Office to approve the envelope or mailing side of the postcard.

- Easy to read text: no fancy spirals, not too small a typeface
- Minimal font varieties: Fine-tuning with fonts brings balance to the design.
- White space is good, enabling people to read and comprehend more easily.
- Use one dominant item; this could be an image, headline copy or logo.
- Have a call to action: Come to my web site, come to my open studio.
- Recognizable logo: If they like you and connect your logo with your art, they will look at the mailer.

REMEMBER

- First and foremost, don't make your piece look like junk mail.
- Get attention through design, mailer size and words.
- Make them an offer: Invite them to your studio, give them a discount.
- Over-deliver: Offer to deliver and hang your pieces.
- Mail at least three times a year to your 20%.

INNOVATION

To make his one-color brochure into a four-color piece, one clever artist pasted his four-color business card onto the front cover in the framed area he had printed with his computer. I could hardly tell that it was a business card. It looked and felt like it was printed right on the paper.

POSTCARDS

Hand out postcards of your artwork like business cards.

Inventive cards

As in most promotions, it pays to be creative. You want people to keep your postcards? How about an oversized postcard that people can post on their bulletin board or use as a poster? Make your promo piece hard to toss into the wastebasket. Make it valuable enough that the recipient will keep it.

- You don't necessarily have to have four-color postcards printed for an exhibition or opening announcement. I've seen some beautifully designed one-, two- and three-color cards. These days, however, there is not a huge difference in cost for four-color printing.
- Card stock does not have to be the conventional 10pt. With paper prices rising, lighter-weight stock such as 8pt is common and fulfills postal requirements.
- Standard 4x6" postcards can get your artwork's image across, but being a bit more inventive may win you much longer viewing. Make an 11x7" postcard (it costs more to mail) and get a lot more space on a bulletin board.
- Attract more attention and create a more lasting memory by sending a Happy Thanksgiving card instead of a Christmas card. Or how about a Happy Summer card!

Postcard printers

If you decide to print four-color postcards with images of your artwork, the Internet is the place to find a printer; you can't beat the prices and convenience. Don't expect a "perfect" color match, but it will be very close to the original. We found that GotPrint at www.gotprint.com has by far the best prices, as well as quick turnaround.

For small quantity mailings, you can keep printing costs down by using your personal desktop color printer.

Postcard deck

If you belong to an organization, your group could compile a card deck. It will attract more attention than an individual postcard and have about 10-25 postcards inside. Each artist prints her own 4x6" postcard, and all are compiled within a clear envelope (so you see an image when you receive it; not a bland white envelope). Mailing costs are divided by all. It's hard for people not to be curious about this package and to open it! Order clear envelopes from www.clearenvelopes.com.

TAKING A RISK

An artist sent 1000 fancy direct-mail brochures to a specific area near where he lived—a very high-income residential area. In not too long a time, he had made two big sales—his originals sell for $9000—as well as evoked some interest from other potential clients.

The factors that made his mailing different from most are:

- ★ An exquisite brochure—11x17" folded in half and inserted in an envelope. The brochure probably cost $1-2. He received this well-designed brochure free from his publisher.
- ★ This artist was known in the area. He had been the poster artist for a recent, well-known art fair. He was also part of a well-respected gallery in town, a gallery that hadn't sold any of his work for ages. The gallery advertisements included his name, however, and his name was first on a long list because his last name begins with the letter "A."
- ★ People loved his style of art.

His steady exposure to a particular locale paid off. If he continues to mail to the same people, they will start networking and do his sales and advertising by word-of-mouth!

This artist took a big risk. However, with all his previous history he made the right, educated choice.

BROCHURES

Until you are quite established, you probably won't have need for an extensive brochure: Your web site acts as that. When you are ready for this format—expensive to design, print and mail—read some tips on proper formatting and design at www.artmarketing.com/downloads.html.

MAILING LISTS

Organize your list on the computer. MicrosoftPro is a great software program for keeping track of databases.

From the start of your decision to become an entrepeneur, you will be building your in-house mailing list. You will use this list throughout your career; guard it closely. Try to contact everyone on this list at least once a year. The aim is not to have the biggest list, but the best—the most specific list for your personal marketing needs.

You already have a list in your personal phone book to start with: family, friends, doctor, dentist, bookkeeper, insurance agent and all the other professionals you deal with. Add to your list:

Architects	Arts councils	Art critics	Art organizations
Businesses	Collectors	Galleries	Interior designers
Museums	Publishers	Publications/editors	

Just think of it: If you have 100 people on your list of potential customers and you sold one painting a month to those people, it would take just eight years for all of them to become buyers!

Research

Research is an essential ingredient for all businesses. While you do your research, both online and off, you will be adding potential buyers, including art professionals and private individuals, to your list.

- Go through your local Yellow Pages to find the names of galleries, publishers, Realtors, art organizations in your locale.
- Browse the Internet for potential clients—fine-art consultants, corporate art consultants, licensing agents, art publishers, greeting card publishers. Review their web sites to find out what style of artwork each works with.
- Include acquaintances as well as attendees of previous exhibitions and open studios you have held.
- Browse through art periodicals to see what types of work galleries are selling; add appropriate galleries.

Coding

It's important to code the names on your list in such a manner that you can pull out the specific group of people you want for a particular mailing.

Code 5 = purchaser	Code 4 = attended opening	Code 3 = potential client
Code 2 = wishy-washy	Code 1 = not very active	

Also have a code for genres of professional:

88 = galleries	77 = consultants	66 = interior designers
55 = museums	44 = press	33 = friends

RENTING LISTS

When you are successful with your in-house list, it could be time to branch out. You might be ready to rent a list.

Do research before you rent a list. Who have you had the best sales with: art consultants, interior designers, galleries? When you figure this out, you can decide on an appropriate list to rent.

Patron lists from your local museum could be a very effective contact list to begin with, especially if you're somewhat known about town and these people are already familiar with your name.

- Interior design organizations such as www.iida.org and www.asid.org rent their member lists, sometimes by geographic area.
- Most trade shows sell lists of attendees. Contact them directly or try VAN list at www.visualartnetwork.com.

If you refer to your target market chart and decide on some specific genre you would like to approach, there is probably a mailing list available of people who purchase this genre.

Art World Mailing Lists www.artmarketing.com
ArtNetwork rents lists of art world professionals nationwide: corporate art consultants, galleries, interior designers, architects and more (as well as providing e-mail blasts to art world professionals).

America Business Info www.listbazaar.com
Mailing lists acquired from the Yellow Pages

Standard Rate and Data www.srds.com
A list broker for almost every genre

World Innovators www.worldinnovators.com
A list broker for many genres

IT'S IN THE MAIL

by Michael Anthony Cheatham

Artists usually find the marketing part of being an artist to be a drag. We would rather spend our time designing and creating. That's why I have been exploring direct mail marketing. Direct mail marketing has proven to allow me time for creating while still reaching important buyers. Here's how I personally do it.

Promotional piece

First you need something to mail! Don't choose an expensive catalog for the first mailer. It's not cost-effective. To stay within my budget, I use postcards. On the front is a photo of my jewelry. On the back is a list of all the major places that carry my work, as well as my URL and phone number.

Target group

Who is the best group of people for purchasing the product that I am selling? Is it galleries, museum stores, private individuals? Figuring out who your target market is takes a little research. Upon deciding which group of people would be best to mail to, I need to find out how to get their names. I could start with the phone book. If I want people outside my immediate area, I could go to the library and use the phone books from across the country. I could look for a company that rents lists. For my first try, I found that ArtNetwork had the exact list I needed—gift store buyers at museums.

Third time's a charm: the 1-2-3 rule

Don't expect immediate results from just one mailing; most people mistakenly do! The mailing industry will tell you that it takes three "hits" in order to entice buyers. This became clear to me when I took this advice and did three mailings. Each time I had better results.

I chose a variation on my first postcard for the second mailing, adding some new museums to the back copy. For the third mailing, I again had a slightly different postcard. You want to keep your mailer recognizable so that the receiver associates it with your previous mailings. I plan to mail to this same group every 3-6 months. To get the attention of busy people, you have to knock loudly and persistently at their door. Your artwork must be kept in front of them. Through consistent mailings, I have been able to show this group my evolution as an artist and my consistency as a jeweler. They will take notice of the other galleries or museums where I am currently showing. Galleries don't want to be left behind. They see all the hip places currently displaying my work, and they want to display it too.

Collecting funds

Most of my work is sold on consignment—I receive no monies until the piece is sold. If a gallery expresses interest in consigning my work, we sign a "consignment agreement." I research through their local Better Business Bureau and Chamber of Commerce to see if there have been any complaints reported about them. I also ask them for names of other artists who are working with them on consignment. I call these artists to ask them if the company pays on time. All orders are sent registered, insured, with a return receipt for verification.

Museums tend to buy up-front, rarely taking consignment. In this case, I ask for prepayment on the first two orders. Additional orders are billed at 30 days net or, better yet, paid by PayPal.

❧

Michael Anthony Cheatham is a lapidary, jeweler and silversmith. He resides in southern California. He received his Gemologist Diploma from The Gemological Institute of America/GIA in Carlsbad, CA.

E-NEWSLETTERS

To send an e-blast to your in-house list, use Vertical Response or Constant Contact.

Many companies these days use e-mail newsletters as a way to update clients on their business happenings. You probably receive e-newsletters and ads every day. Save the ones that you like and have your designer use them as models when you are ready to create your own e-newsletter.

SUBJECT LINES

Developing a strong subject line for an e-mail blast is the most important factor. If you cannot entice a viewer to open the e-mail, you've lost him before you've begun. Look at e-mail blasts that draw your attention, and study why they do so. Is it a particular word or "device" they've used? Spend some time developing your subject line; it will be worth the effort.

WORDS THAT WORK

Discount	Easy	How to	Last chance
New	Guaranteed	Proven	Powerful
Quick	Save		

NUMBERS THAT WORK

15 Reasons to	9 Ways to	4 Secrets to	6 Strategies You've

TIPS

- Put a tip or hint in the newsletter that will entice the recipient to keep it: How to clean a frame, where to store unframed works.
- Note new purchases by customers. People love to see their name in print. (Get permission first.)
- Note any experiences with customers you might want to share. Did one of your patrons have a show for you at her house? Let the other customers know how fun it was. Maybe you will get other patrons to offer their home for your next show.
- Know your purpose: to inform, sell, inspire
- Know your goal: to create interest in your work

E-MAIL BLASTS

Eflux www.e-flux.com

Art & Education www.artandeducation.net

It's Liquid www.www.itsliquid.com

ArtNetwork www.artmarketing.com/e-mailblasts.html

Chapter 6

Advertising

Ad placement

Artist directories

A master-passion is the love of news.
George Crabbe

AD PLACEMENT

It's said that it takes the average consumer nine exposures before a product is remembered. Whenever you plan to advertise, you must follow the "golden rule" and do it a minimum of three times in the same magazine or newspaper.

25-25-50 RULE

In a group of 100 people, 25 will like you, 25 will dislike you and 50 won't care. Don't waste your time on the 25 who don't like you or the 50 who don't care. Concentrate all your promotional activities on the 25 who like you.

The approach to advertising for an individual artist is different from other types of businesses. Selling original artwork directly through an ad is generally difficult. Galleries that advertise in magazines such as *ArtNews* and *Art in America* have megabucks in their ad budget. These galleries are thinking of long-term promotion and the gallery's general reputation, not just the individual show they are promoting. Galleries that don't represent well-recognized artists can't afford to advertise in these expensive venues.

Advertising in your local newspaper or magazine does not generally bring a lot of sales. People do not buy art through an advertisement unless the artist is already known to them. If your aim is not sales but recognition, leading to sales later, then advertising could be a way to go.

One big-name artist analyzes the effectiveness of his magazine advertising in this manner: If he generates enough income just to pay for the ad itself, then the ad is worthwhile. He gains exposure and, soon, word-of-mouth will bring profits. People have seen his ad so many times that it's finally sinking in. He looks well established; thus he gains respect. That's when his ad really begins to work. If you start to advertise, you must be willing to make a long-term investment. Otherwise your money is essentially lost.

TAKING RISKS IS PART OF BEING AN ENTREPRENEUR

One artist rented a billboard for two months in his small town. He painted on it for four hours daily. By the time he was done, everyone in town knew his name and his style! Not only had they seen his work on the billboard, but he had major write-ups in the local press as well as national newspapers. Galleries called him. He took a risk and it worked!

❧

Another artist put her art images on a software program that plays them as a screen saver. She gives away this screen saver to customers and potential clients.

Advertising is not direct sales; it is mostly name recognition, which will ultimately lead to direct sales. Study the publication you are going to be advertising in before you commit your bucks. Are other artists advertising? If so, how do they exhibit their work?

The golden rule of advertising is repetition.

Cardinal rules in advertising

- Frequency and repetition
- Stand-out ad
- Emotional, exciting (not only factual) ad
- Simple layout, to the point
- Targeted audience
- Timing
- Repeating logo
- Proper information: telephone, directions, name, web site, e-mail

Word-of-mouth advertising

Word-of-mouth will be your best advertiser. Word-of-mouth advertising is what will start occurring once you have reached enough people in a given community. If a customer is to refer you to another potential client, of course you must have happy customers.

- Ask for a referral from a purchaser or a friend to add to your list. If someone really likes your work, she will be more than happy to give you a lead to a friend or business associate.
- Give a little extra and people will start talking about you. Install a piece of artwork at someone's home and there are bound to be stories about "the artist."
- The best salesperson for any item is a happy buyer. Pleased customers validate your work.

ARTIST DIRECTORIES

If you place an ad in one of these directories, check to see if you can get reprints of your page. A reprint is an exact duplicate of your page (usually blank on the reverse side). You can use it as a flyer or give-away at your next show.

These advertising venues display a typical piece of an artist's work, along with contact information, giving artists exposure to fine-art professionals they otherwise might never reach.

DIRECTORIES

Artist Advocate www.artistadvocatemagazine.com
Quarterly publication with half- or full-page ads for artists

Black Book www.blackbook.com
Mostly for illustrators

Direct Art Magazine www.slowart.com
Fine-art ads sent to galleries

Directory of Illustration www.directoryofillustration.com
Mostly for illustrators

Guidebook of Art www.aotw.com
Art of the West magazine

New American Paintings www.newamericanpaintings.com
A series of six regional books, published annually, showcasing fine artists

Workbook www.workbook.com
Mostly for illustrators

One artist living in Florida advertised her work in a publication. She was surprised to receive a call one day from a collector in Texas. He had fallen in love with the piece in the ad. Within two weeks, he flew into Miami just to view the painting and to verify that it looked like the picture in the book. He left Miami the next morning, having paid the artist for the piece as well as for shipping to Texas. There was no indecision on the collector's part—just pure and simple love. When someone falls in love with your painting, it is truly the biggest compliment in the world. "It all happened so quickly. It was such an exciting event," says the artist. She went on to say that this was the most unusual, dreamlike experience that she has ever encountered in all her years of marketing her art.

Chapter 7

Public Art

Publicly-funded programs

Working with nonprofits

Museums

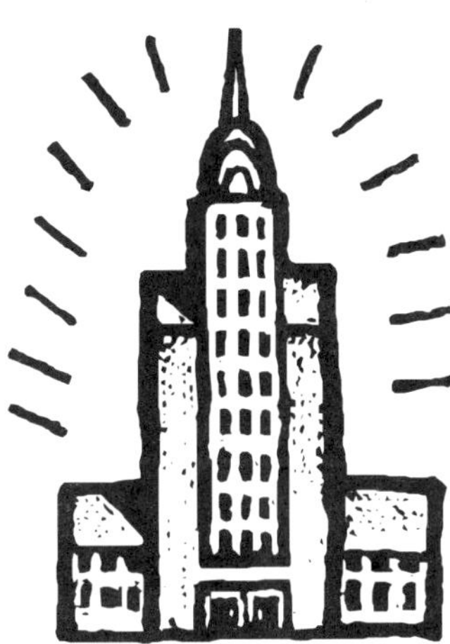

The superior man is modest in his speech but exceeds in his actions.
Confucius

PUBLICLY-FUNDED PROGRAMS

How to sell to the public art arena is a mystery to most artists.

Art councils

Arts councils are funded by more than 350 federal, state, county and city governments across America, as well as by private donation. Arts councils were created to bring more art into the general public's view: performing art, visual art, and music. As a visual artist, it's important to get to know your local arts council's visual art director. She can be helpful to your career, leading to local collectors, possible exhibition venues, recommendations of all sorts. She, of course, wants to know that you are a serious artist and have quality work. Arts councils often sponsor seminars, have gallery space available to artists, and keep slide registries. Arts councils sometimes sponsor talks about how to acquire a public art commission: www.racc.org/resources/5110-racc-workshop-howd-you-get-public-art-gig.

Percentage-for-the-Arts program

Most arts councils have a "Percentage-for-the-Arts" program. This is a program that requires a percentage of the construction budget of any new public building to be put toward art. In California, many counties require 1% to be set aside; in some, as much as 2%. Sometimes called an "Art-in-Public-Places Program," it is meant to enhance the environment through works of art. Keep current on "Percentage-for-the-Arts" programs by reading online listings or by calling arts councils directly and asking to be put on their mailing list for future commission possibilities.

Selection procedures for "Percentage-for-the-Arts" programs vary. They may include:

- Direct purchase by jury or panel
- Invitational projects. By using a slide registry or other means, the panel selects one artist to draw up a proposal, and if it is accepted, the artist receives the commission.
- Limited competition. Several artists are invited to compete.
- Open competition

For sculptors of large outdoor pieces, a little investigation into public art venues is well worth the effort. Other media appropriate to public viewing, both in- and outdoors, are also needed; more than 20% of public art is two-dimensional.

Slide banks

A slide bank, also known as a slide registry, is a file of images (sometimes digital these days) that is used as a resource for public art committees, art consultants, companies or private individuals interested in commissioning specific media for a project.

- All slide banks work differently; some charge artists a fee to be listed, but most are free.
- Some slide banks are juried, some are not.

Putting your work into a slide bank makes your work accessible to many public art programs. Read more about slide banks at www.ncarts.org/elements/docs/Slide Registries.pdf and at www.findarticles.com/p/articles/mi_m1546/is_n6_v9/ai_16646679.

President Clinton was presented with a silkscreen of Roy Lichtenstein's "Composition III" by Friends of Art and Preservation in Embassies/FAPE. The signed and numbered edition of 175 was donated to FAPE and the "Art in the Embassies Program." Prints are placed in each of the US Embassies worldwide. Can you imagine what publicity over the years this will bring Lichtenstein?

Some slide banks

- www.artistsregister.com
- www.urbanartinstitute.org
- www.communityarts.net
- www.artistsspace.org
- www.utahpublicart.org
- www.ct.gov/cct/cwp/view.asp?a=2207&Q=299724
- www.tempe.gov/arts/PublicArt/ArtistSlidebank.htm
- www.artsnashville.org/pubartprojects/ebgw/ebgw.php
- www.whitecolumns.org

What do I have to submit?

Submission requirements vary, but, of course, you will need to have images and a bio. Often a statement or letter of intent is also needed. Once you have public projects under your belt, your application will be looked at more intently. But remember, the 20-year-old artist who was attending Harvard is the one who won the competition for the public art piece inWashington, DC for the Vietnam War Memorial. Maya Lin still has a flourishing association with public art throughout the US.

Sometimes you will have to come up with a preliminary proposal for a project. Sometimes proposals are requested only from those artists who are considered finalists. Sometimes "honorariums" are awarded for the work on a proposal. You must describe your concept, what materials will be used, how it will be constructed and maintained; develop a time-line and budget; and include drawings and sometimes scale models. The artist applying rarely does all the work himself; he often enlists a variety of people to help.

The Artist's Guide to Public Art: How to Find and Win Commissions by Lynn Basa is an excellent guide to this genre and is a must-read if you are going into this area.

Working with an administrator

Administrators are generally more familiar with the public art process than the artist. They are there to assist the artist and answer questions when needed.

When designing public art, one needs to address the particular needs of the public. For instance, when creating art for a cruise line, you would want to talk to baggage handlers, passengers, cruise line employees, and administrators, and learn everything you possibly can about the facility.

Pursuing leads

- Art magazines often have a "Call for Entries" noting upcoming projects.
- Get your name on e-mail lists to be notified of any upcoming competitions for your local and statewide agencies.
- www.4culture.org
- www.callforentry.org
- www.theartlist.com
- www.artopportunities.org
- www.artdeadline.com
- www.artopportunitiesmonthly.com
- www.public-art-directory.com

Periodicals

Competitions www.competitions.org
Focuses on architectural and landscape competitions

Public Art Review www.publicartreview.org

Public Art Network/PAN

Public Art Network/PAN is the only professional network in the United States dedicated to the field of public art. As a program of Americans for the Arts, PAN advocates for policies that serve communities creating public art. The PAN network brings together artists, community members, and art and design professionals through online resources, professional development and education opportunities, knowledge-sharing practices, and strategic partnerships. www.artsusa.org/networks/public_art_network/default_002.asp

Cityarts

Cityarts is a 33-year-old organization that produces community art—sculpture, murals and mosaics. Professional artists and community members collaborate on various projects in and around the five boroughs of New York. www.cityarts.org

Art-in-Embassies program/AIEP

Though many citizens have never heard of it, **AIEP** is over 30 years old! Placements are made in US Embassy offices and homes around the world, providing excellent exposure for artwork to various dignitaries, including political, government and state officials. Work must be available for travel for three years and is often purchased at the end of the loan period. www.state.gov

Art-in-Architecture/AIA

The General Services Administration and the Department of Veterans Affairs, both federal agencies, have **AIA** programs for their buildings nationwide. They maintain their own slide registries. **AIA** commissions the nation's leading artists to create large-scale works of art for new federal buildings. These artworks enhance the civic meaning of federal architecture and showcase the vibrancy of American visual arts.

GSA reserves one-half of one percent of the estimated construction cost of each new federal building to commission artists. A panel comprised of art professionals, civic and community representatives, and the project's lead design architect meet to discuss opportunities for artists to participate in the building project. This panel reviews a diverse pool of artist candidates and nominates finalists for GSA to evaluate. Artists who receive federal commissions work with the project architects as members of a design team to ensure that the artworks are meaningfully integrated into the overall project.

GSA maintains a large registry of artists interested in being considered for federal commissions. This registry is the principal resource for the panels that assist GSA in selecting artists for each new project. www.gsa.gov

DEFENESTRATION

An abandoned building located at 214 6th St (at Howard St) in San Francisco has been infiltrated by hanging sofas, desks, light fixtures and more. Most peope driving by probably don't even notice it, and it's not because it's uninteresting. Defenestration takes place on the second through fourth stories of this corner building. All the pieces are recycled: Who'd want to hang a new refrigerator out of an abandoned building? Exactly how the artist—Brian Goggin—got the furniture up there? Well, that's part of the mystery, probably never to be solved. www.metaphorm.org www.defenestration.org

When creating public art, you will most likely be in the elements—outdoors, where you will be observed by the public. If you're not open to that and don't think you can cope with it, don't do this type of project.

Sculpture parks

There are magnificent sculpture parks in almost every state, some private (but open to the public) and some run by museums or other organizations. These parks often have exhibitions and competitions allowing sculptors to expose sculptural work for extended periods of time, as well as purchase pieces for their permanent collections. Your best resource is www.artnut.com.

Murals

Murals have been in existence since the caveman started doodling on walls. Graffiti artists have become mainstream and even get commissions to create murals to improve community buildings.

Both Los Angeles's and New York City's mass transit systems have growing collections of permanent and temporary art, including murals. There are indoor and outdoor murals, Renaissance and modern. Some are by renowned artists, others emerging. You will find murals on huge outdoor city water tanks and backyard propane tanks, from the Sistine Chapel (134x44 feet) to the Long Beach sea mural by Wyland. Apprenticing with a muralist might be a good way to start to understand the business.

Mural organizations

- **The Social and Public Art Resource Center** www.sparcmurals.org
- **Precita Eyes Muralists** www.precitaeyes.org
- **Mural Arts Program** www.muralarts.org
- **Mural Conservancy of Los Angeles** www.lamurals.org
- **Arts for Transit** www.mta.info/mta/aft
- **Chicago Public Art Group** www.cpag.net
- **National Society of Mural Painters** www.nationalsocietyofmuralpainters.com

Mosaics

Mosaics have been a popular medium since the Renaissance and are used quite often in the public domain; they are durable and beautiful. Kiki St Phalle was a leading innovator in the field. See her Tarot Garden near Florence, Italy (www.tarotgarden.com) and Queen Califia's Magical Circle Garden in Escondido, CA (www.queencalifia.org).

MOSAIC ORGANIZATIONS AND SCHOOLS

- **Society of American Mosaic Artists** www.americanmosaics.org
- **Chicago Mosaic School** www.chicagomosaicschool.com
- **Institute of Mosaic Art** www.instituteofmosaicart.com

PHILLY MAGIC GARDEN

If there is one present-day artist dedicated to mosaics, it is Isaiah Zagar in Philadelphia. When you visit his site (either online or in person), you will view an awesome creation throughout the streets that he lives on. Almost solely, he has renovated this section of town and turned it into a tourist attraction. His grassroots attempt to introduce the general public to beauty via his mosaic creations has really taken off.

Magic Gardens is a folk art environment, a gallery space, and a nonprofit organization. It is a fully mosaiced indoor gallery and a massive outdoor labyrinth of mosaic sculpture primarily consisting of found objects. Half a city block is covered with a myriad of tile, texture and color. A walk through the streets will reveal sculptures made from bicycle wheels, hand-made tiles and mirrors of every shape and size.

Zagar has devoted himself to beautifying the South Street neighborhood since the late 1960s, when he moved to the area with his wife Julia. The couple helped spur the revitalization of the area by purchasing and renovating derelict buildings, adding colorful mosaics on both their private and public walls. Zagar started working on the Magic Gardens in 1994 in the vacant lot near his studio. He began by constructing a massive fence to protect the area from harm and then spent the next 14 years excavating tunnels and grottoes, sculpting multilayered walls, and tiling and grouting the 3,000-square-foot space. The installation pays tribute to Zagar's many artistic influences, as well as the events and experiences of his life. Self-guided or guided tours are available. Julia's still-thriving folkart store—The Eyes Gallery—is located at 402 South St. His son produced a video of Isaiah in 2008—*In a Dream*. www.phillymagicgardens.org www.eyesgallery.com

---

WORKING WITH NONPROFITS

These days, many nonprofit organizations work together with artists in their promotional efforts—Sierra Club, Harlem Theatre, KQED TV, Little League, Brooklyn Art Museum, and many thousands more across the nation. For all involved, this becomes a win win situation. The key is to find the right organization for your style of artwork.

Selecting a nonprofit

I constantly advocate to artists, "You don't need a gallery to make it as an artist." It has been proven to me once again that this philosophy is sound. I was recently told an innovative way to work with a nonprofit charitable organization. Think about the following method and adapt it to your own artwork, your own needs.

- Find a nonprofit (Yes, you pick it!) that you would like to work with, one whose cause you feel passionate about (cancer research, animal shelter, AIDS, whales, the rain forest). Since you will be networking amongst their most active constituents, it is important that you learn a little history about the organization, as well as its mission.
- After studying the organization's history, prepare a simple outline of your project idea in writing. Eventually you will be proposing this well-thought-out idea to someone at the organization; you might be sending the proposal in writing. Brainstorm with yourself, friends and family about your various ideas and get their feedback, especially for your first proposal.

Proposing a fundraising event

Most charitable foundations have an annual or semiannual fundraiser. Offer to help raise funds by auctioning a painting, selling prints and having a gala. Propose that the nonprofit buy an artwork of yours to auction; you give them a 50% discount off your retail price. Chances are they will sell it for the retail amount, and hopefully more. Along with offering the organization one of your beautiful originals, you can offer them the onetime right to reproduce a print of it, for a fee—a royalty. Of course, this fee will depend on the number of prints they plan to produce. Include the image's usage for their postcard or invitation free of charge.

If, for instance, they are a 5000-member organization, perhaps they have 500 active members. This is the type of information you will need to find out in order to make a valid proposal to them. If the above stats are correct, they could easily estimate to sell 100 posters, perhaps even 200-300 or more depending on the price. Remember: Members know this is a fundraiser and are more easily persuaded to purchase. Perhaps they can plan to use the unsold posters as a promotional gift to new members who join the following year.

Let's say they plan to print 300 posters. They plan to sell them for $25. You have also suggested they print limited-edition giclées—25 signed and numbered at $150.

That's a total of $11,500 (300x$25=$7500 and 25x$150=$3750) income value. You should request approximately 10% of that or $1125 for reproduction rights.

The fundraising event could be a Sunday afternoon tea with strawberries and cream, costing each participant $25-50; it could be a sit-down dinner at $250 a seat.

Consider in your proposal what they have succeeded with in the past and who their constituents are—that is, what they can afford and what they would like. One of the main draws of your offering is an auction. They will be receiving 50% of all your sales from the exhibition, the same percentage that a gallery normally takes as a commission. If your paintings sell for $1200-$3000 and you sell four paintings during this event, for a total of $10,000, $5000 would go to the organization and $5000 to you.

In your proposal, you might suggest they hire an experienced art salesperson for the evening. Perhaps they will only go for part of your proposal. You will have a guestbook out and will meet many potential patrons, patrons who could become long-term customers for you.

Before you present your final proposal to them, make sure you do some research.

- How much money do they usually raise?
- How much do they ideally want to raise?
- What kind of event do they normally have?
- How many members do they presently have? How many are active?
- What is their mission statement?
- How long have they been around?
- Is it a national or local organization?

Be sure to show them actual profit possibilities.

Know your obligations

If both parties are going to benefit, you will both have to make certain efforts. Before you sign up, make sure you both understand what your obligations are. Get the facts down in writing to avoid problems.

Plan to participate with the same nonprofit for several years.

Download a sample press release at www.artmarketing.com/downloads.html.

Press releases

Take an active role in getting press releases out and meeting and inviting the local press. Having the nonprofit's name attached to yours can help you get better publicity.

- Send the press releases on the nonprofit's letterhead.
- Use the nonprofit's bulk mailing permit. Invite people on your mailing list: Perhaps they will become a member of the nonprofit.
- Note the nonprofit as the host and you as a sponsor.

PSAs

PSAs are distributed to general managers of radio stations or community news departments in TV stations to get listed on community calendars. A Public Service Announcement—PSA—is a shorter version of a press release.

- ★ Broadcast media, especially radio stations, give priority to PSAs from nonprofit or community-based organizations. As an artist, your PSA should promote your events as "free and open to the public." This will qualify you for inclusion in the community calendars.

The FCC requires radio and TV stations to air a number of PSAs each day free for nonprofit groups. Compose 15-, 30- and 60-second versions of an announcement about your event. Be concise, focusing on the benefit to the community. Be clear about what the public will receive: You are giving $5 for each sale towards a new animal at the zoo. PSAs should:

- ★ Include one-paragraph write-ups
- ★ Feature the five Ws and How
- ★ Have contact information
- ★ Include the first paragraph of your press release
- ★ Be printed on your letterhead or e-mailed with your logo

❧

The above was excerpted from Chapter 5 of *Power Up with PR* by Jackie Abramian, available at www.artmarketing.com.

SAMPLE PROFIT SCHEDULE

Nonprofit's income	
300 prints @ $25	$7,500
25 signed giclées @ $150	3,750
Tea party income (100x$30)	3,000
Auction income	7,000
Subtotal	**$21,250**
Nonprofit's expenses	
Printing costs	$ 5,000
Image usage	1,125
Auction artwork	1,500
Purchased artwork	2,000
Total expenses	**$(9,625)**
Total profit for organization	**$11,625**
Artist's income	
Original artwork for auction	$ 3,500
Image usage	1,125
Total profit for artist	**$ 4,625**

In the above scenario, one piece was auctioned for $3000; two pieces were sold for $2000 each.

Think into the future. If this event is successful for both parties, it could become an annual event.

FOLLOW-UP

- Send press releases after the event to let the public know how much they helped; state how much was raised and what it will be used for, along with photographs of the event.
- Send thank-you notes to everyone involved.
- Create a mailing list of people who came to the event. Add these people to your personal list. Send a postcard to them when you have an open studio or an exhibition at a local gallery. Treat them as your potential clients.

CASES IN POINT

An artist called me one day to ask for a short consultation. He wanted to know what I thought of an idea he had. He wanted to take a painting he had created (which I had never seen) to a meeting of the Brothers of the Temple, an organization similar to the Elks Club. He wanted to raise funds for prints of this piece by having members of the organization buy prints at a special pre-publication price. He thought the members would like his painting enough to participate in this venture. I thought it was an innovative approach. Two weeks later, he called back to report the news. He had arranged to do a sales pitch at their meeting, bringing the original artwork. Not only did the members buy enough pre-publication prints to support his printing, leaving him with several hundred copies more to sell, but they bought the original painting as well. What a coup! I told him to keep up the good work and find another, similar organization, create another painting, and do the same sales pitch. Take the ball and run with it!

❧

Another artist liked to do historical paintings. She took it upon herself to do a large mural-type painting of her town's history, which she had studied thoroughly. After completing the piece, she decided to try to sell it to her City Council. After much red tape, prints were made by the City Council and sold as a fundraiser for which she received a nice royalty, and they eventually bought her piece (due to her lack of experience, without a signed agreement) for a price less than what she had thought they originally agreed upon. All in all, though, this venture was a great success. She made a royalty on the prints, got great publicity in the town, sold her original work and had extra prints to sell on her own. Her job then was to go to the next township and propose a similar fundraising event to them, promoting the success of her first fundraiser. This time she would make sure she had a signed contract from the start.

❧

Sculptor Richard MacDonald donated a 22-foot monument portraying an Olympic gymnast to the state of Georgia for the 1996 games. He took full advantage of this opportunity and received a lot of free publicity. I'm certain he also got many sales. A great investment in the long-term goals of his career!

MUSEUMS

A great way to meet collectors is to become a member of your local museum and volunteer your time.

Museum curators spend millions of dollars on artwork throughout their careers. Some pieces are purchased at auctions, some from private dealers and collectors, some directly from artists. Museums generally own work from both living and non-living artists. Exhibitions are created from their permanent collection with borrowed works added. Sometimes they even rent an entire exhibition.

Get to know your local curators by becoming a museum member and attending openings. Remember, "infiltration" is a slow, organic process. Eventually you can invite a museum curator to your studio or an opening.

Approaching a museum

You can approach a museum to sell a piece, donate a piece or have an exhibit. You need to be well-prepared if you approach them as an emerging artist. Do you have a really great theme for an exhibition? Smaller museums will be much more open to emerging artists. To approach a museum:

- Write a brief letter of introduction to the appropriate curator.
- Include your resume, promotional materials, announcements from solo shows, and six to 10 photo prints of your work.
- When approaching a museum, remember they are looking for innovative exhibits with a great theme.

Smaller museums around the US

Sometimes smaller, local museums purchase work from emerging artists. They are also more likely to exhibit local or emerging artists. Do some research online for museums in your area and approach them when your work is in an upward momentum.

- A list of small museums can be viewed at www.art-collecting.com/museums.htm.
- **Orange County Museum of Art** www.ocma.net
- **Napa Valley Museum** www.napavalleymuseum.org
- **The Aldrich Contemporary Art Museum** www.aldrichart.org
- **Jersey City Museum** www.jerseycitymuseum.org
- **Newark Museum** www.newarkmuseum.org
- **Katonah Museum of Art** www.katonahmuseum.org
- **Hudson River Museum** www.hrm.org
- **Bronx Museum** www.bronxmuseum.org

Exhibits

If you are thinking of approaching a museum for an exhibit, remember that they are not places that sell; they simply exhibit artwork. Exhibiting work in a museum, however, can be a great boost to your career. Your credibility will increase tenfold. Receptions are usually held for patrons of the museum; you, of course, will attend and introduce yourself to these patrons. You will meet curators and other museum staff as well.

- Many museums have annual competitions for emerging artists. These could be your best bet for introduction.
- Some museums have rental galleries (see page 113). This is an excellent way to find new clients, also.
- To locate museums out of your area, ask your librarian for a museum directory: *Official Museum Directory* and *Museums of the World International Directory of the Arts* are two. If you have a specialty—equine, wildlife, florals, historical—look for this genre of museum.

Traveling exhibitions

Sometimes museums work with companies that create and rent exhibits. Go to www.museummarketplace.com and type in "Traveling Exhibition Organizations" or "Providers" to find more places to research.

Smith Kramer www.smithkramer.com

Curatorial Assistance www.curatorial.com

Exhibits USA www.eusa.org

Museums are looking for quality work. In recent years, their budgets have shrunk. They can no longer afford to buy consistently the number-one, superstar artists. They are looking for emerging artists they can afford, whose worth will grow with time.

Curatorial consultants

Curatorial consultants create exhibits, often for a particular museum or center, and often with a particular theme in mind. They are always keeping their eyes open for innovative styles. Introducing curatorial consultants to your work might open doors to their exhibits.

- **Paragon Research Associates** www.paragonresearch.net
- **Suzette McAvoy** www.suzettemcavoy.com

Donations to museums

Storing artwork has become a costly venture for most museums, and, therefore, many museums do not want an unknown artist to approach them about possible donations of artwork. If you are becoming well-known in a particular area of the country, however, their attitude might be different.

If you donate a piece to a museum, draw up a contract. Make it clear that you still own the reproduction rights to the donated piece.

Make the most of a donation

- Ask the curator if you can have a formal unveiling.
- Invite the press to the event.
- Be sure to list that you are in the museum collection on your resume.

Fundraisers

At some point in your career, you will probably be asked to donate a piece of artwork to a museum fundraiser (or some other charity). Auctions have been used for decades to gather money for nonprofits.

But what about the artist who is donating? Is it so great for him? The first few inquiries you receive for a donation will pump up your ego. When you become known for giving in your community, however, you might receive as many as five calls a month for donations. At some point you will have to set limits.

Requirements

- Set a bottom limit on your auction price. If it doesn't sell for that minimum, you receive it back.
- You must be informed of the price it sold for, as well as the buyer's name and contact info.
- The organization must pay for framing and transportation.
- You receive a percentage of the auction price.
- You receive two free tickets to the event.

Tips

- If you decide to participate for your favorite cause, don't give them the least popular of your pieces. It will come back to haunt you and is not good publicity.
- Why would you want to donate a piece to an auction? One possible perk could be a catalog with a full color image, which you can use to promote yourself.

What nonprofits neglect to consider when asking for donations to art auctions is that artists who are not paid a percentage of the auction price for their donation may often donate second-rate work.

One artist donated a piece to a large museum in the South. They gave her artwork a special unveiling. The museum got the press to come, which published several stories on her work. Her piece has since been rotated to different spots in the museum, but for some time it was at the central entrance to the museum. Her next step was to make prints and sell them to the gift shop as well as around town. Her originals became much easier to get into local galleries at that point. She had become known locally.

❧

One artist I know has his photographs traveling to many museums all over the country. He solicits museums with a well-prepared press kit. He is paid to exhibit, and the museum packages and ships his work to the next museum on the list. He also sells cards and posters of his work. (The museum gets a cut). It's a win win situation.

❧

One artist wanted to have a traveling exhibit of her work, which she volunteered free to any museum that would accept it. She only asked that they pay for transportation and her personal expenses for attending the opening. She would also give demonstrations of her work for several days during the exhibition. The response was so successful that she actually had to refuse some museums that wanted to be on her tour!

Chapter 8

Reps and Consultants

Art reps

Art consultants

Approaching art consultants

Set decorators

Private collectors

All children are artists. The trick is to remain an artist and grow up.
Pablo Picasso

ART REPS

Those who learn to take care of their own interests usually surpass the achievements of those who turn their affairs over to others.

An art rep is an individual who generally takes on no more than five to 10 artists and represents their work to specific companies, galleries, publishers and individuals. Sometimes a gallery acts in this capacity, or sometimes the wife, relative or friend of an artist. Most artists fantasize about having a rep. In the last several years, repping an artist has become a more recognized profession in the art world. It appears that in the near future, the fine-art representative will be a more common figure. For the right person, it is a lucrative and satisfying career. They often get 33-50% commission on sales they make; some work by the hour or project.

"Where can I find a rep?" is one of the most common questions I hear from artists. Finding an active art rep can be a dream-come-true for a fine artist. Having a rep, ideally, means that an artist can concentrate on the creation of art instead of dividing time between creation and marketing. Locating a good rep takes time. Often a rep doesn't want to take on an artist who has no sales record or reputation, so you may need to do some footwork and get established first.

BROKERS

A broker is a person who connects a buyer and seller, perhaps at a trade show or through former connections. This person does a lot of networking. An auction house is sometimes considered a broker. Commission varies from 15-50%.

DEALERS

A dealer has many connections in the art world and buys and sells works privately or possibly through a gallery. Commission is usually in the 40-50% range.

MANAGERS

Managers are often paid by the hour. They might do a specific type of job for the artist: bookkeeping, managing contracts, writing contracts or grant proposals, or a variety of these, including public relations.

PUBLICISTS

A publicist is usually hired by the hour or project for promotion of a specific exhibition or museum opening. Often, well-known artists will hire such a person or an entire publicity agency.

ART CONSULTANTS

Always market your uniqueness.

Art consultants, sometimes called corporate art consultants, usually are hired or contracted with by businesses or private individuals to help locate and evaluate works of art. They are in touch with many people and need a variety of art throughout their career. They deal actively in art—it's their livelihood. In today's market, they are the most common go-between for the corporate art collection. They could be involved with new buildings, remodelling, large corporations, book publishers, art publishers, museums, private collectors, galleries, developers and planners, health care, hospitality, and more. They often work with state and federal agencies in the Percentage-for-the-Arts programs. Generally, each consultant has a specialty market with which he deals.

Many art consultants were art history majors in college. They are experienced in the ability to interface with client and artist and know how to orchestrate a project from conception to installation.

- They make studio visits and monitor payment schedules.
- They often take 33-50% commission.

Locating art consultants

- When you see great artwork in some location—library, doctor's office. bank—ask them who helped them choose it.
- Ask your local arts council director if he is familiar with any local art reps.
- Peel-and-stick labels with addresses of corporate art consultants are available at www.artmarketing.com/ML.
- www.artadvisors.org
- www.artsusa.org/pdf/networks/pan/PAN2009_finallist_7-1-09.pdf is a public art consultants list.
- At www.artregister.com and www.artphile.com, you can look up categories such as independent art curators, art consultants, corporate art consultants, art advisors, art services. Do the same kind of search through Google and Yahoo.
- www.artistsonline.biz/services/art_consultant.htm
- If you're looking more in the illustration category, look at www.altpick.com, www.talentworks.com or www.childrensillustrators.com.
- Private Art Dealers Association www.pada.net

Follow art consultants whom you are in contact with on Twitter, LinkedIn or Myspace.

A L C Designs www.alcdesigns.com

Amit May Fine Arts www.amitmay.com

Armstrong Prior Inc www.armstrong-prior.com

Artconnect HQ www.artconnecthq.com

Art4Business www.art4business.com

Art + Service www.kathydowell.com

Art Ability www.artability.com

Art Advice www.artadvice-ny.com/index.html

Art Advisory www.artadvisoryltd.com

Art Advisory Services www.artadvisoryservices.com

Art Advisory Services www.twaas.com

Art Concierge www.locatefineart.squarespace.com

Art Consultants Group www. www.artconsultantsgroup.com

Art Directions www.artdirections.net

Art Environments www.artenviron.com

The Art Partnership www.art-partnership.com

Art Plus www.art-plus.com

Art Source for Design www.artsourcefordesign.com

Art Source LA www.artsourcela.com

Artful City www.artfulcity.com

Artful Solutions www.artfulsolutions.net

Artists Circle www.artistscircleonline.com

Arts Advisory Service www.carolekraus.com

Artsource Consulting www.artsourceinc.com

Artworks www.artworks.com

Blue Tangerine Art www.bluetangerineart.com

Carey Ellis Company www.careyellis.com

Carol Dabb www.cdabbart.com

Corporate Artworks Ltd www.healtheart.com

Dorsey-Hovde Art Design www.dhartdesign.com

DSA Fine Arts www.dsafinearts.com

Easel Art Consulting www.easel-art.com

Fine Art Resources www.fineartresources.com

Fine Arts Advisory www.cristintierney.com

Fine Arts Advisory www.mcqfineart.com/

International Corporate Art www.icart.net

Jean Efron Art Associates www.efronart.com

Joel Straus Consulting www.jsartconsulting.com

Kinzelman Art Consulting www.kinzelmanart.com

Lendrum Fine Art www.lendrumfineart.com

Maria Piscopo www.mpiscopo.com

MFI Art Company www.mfiart.com

Michelle Isenberg & Associates www.misenberg.com

Marc Pally www.marcpally.com

Peak Fine Art Services www.peakfas.com

Saltman Art Associates www.saltmanart.com

Suzy Locke and Associates www.artadvisor.com

Tressa Miller www.tressamiller.com

Vick Corporate Art Advisors www.vickartadvisors.com

Visual Arts Advisory www.visualartsadvisory.com

Visual Arts Consultants www.artconsultation.com

Wendy Kelley Art Advisory www.artworksadvisory.com

Art consultants eventually find you when your marketing puts you out in the public eye.

Approaching Art Consultants

"Should I go with this publisher, rep or gallery?"
If you don't trust a rep, you should never start working with him. Trust your heart and do your research. Go with your gut feeling. You might be wrong, but it's all you really have to go on. If you have any odd feelings about developing a new relationship with anyone in the art world, don't do it!

When professionals work with you, they expect you to be professional. They want artwork finished on time and in accordance with any agreement. Of course, the higher priced your work, the more tolerant they seem to be toward your idiosyncrasies. Once you show them that you mean business by performing well and being timely, they are more likely to call upon you again.

There is a lot of competition to win over corporate art consultants. You must outshine other artists, not only in your artwork but in your professionalism. Be sure to add their names to your mailing list so that you send them notices via mail and e-mail of all your exhibitions. They want to see that you are active and prospering.

When and if you do find a good art consultant, your dealings should occur after you sign a legal agreement (see *Art Office* (www.artmarketing.com) for a variety of legal agreements). Don't think it's going to be a breeze. Pressures inevitably arise.

Work as a team

Even if a consultant is handling your art deals, you will want to keep tabs on what is going on in the art world. So study, research and help your rep.

UNEXPECTED

The Friday evening opening at the Toney Gallery drew its usual crowd of elegantly dressed buyers and aficionados. As I glanced around, I saw someone who looked familiar, but the pieces didn't fit. The friend the man resembled had always defined the term bohemian for me; he did not, as far as I knew, even own a suit. This man was dressed impeccably, custom tailored and slightly European down to his expensive leather shoes and French cuffs and cuff links. I looked again and he caught my eye; he moved toward me, smiling, exuding self-confidence, his hand outstretched in greeting. It was my friend, after all. But what a change! No longer the starving artist, this man looked downright prosperous.

I have known this artist for many years, but this was my first encounter with him in more than 12 months. During this time I had seen no shows or reviews of his work. What had changed? Had he given up art? Had he won the lottery or married an heiress or made a killing in the stock market? We each took a glass of champagne and drifted off to a corner where we could catch up. Yes, there had been a change. And for him it was art consultants.

"I've had one of the best years I've ever had just because of working with art consultants," he told me. He'd given up working with galleries, which was why I had not heard about his art career over the last year. His work was going exclusively to art consultants.

What are art consultants, or, as they are sometimes known, art reps or private art dealers? They are essentially people who sell art but do not have a gallery. They're middlemen who make connections between artists and buyers. And the buyers are very often large-scale buyers. There are hundreds of art consultants throughout the United States, and they handle every kind of art imaginable: from photography to sculpture to paintings to craft.

Art consultants are a curious breed. They're a mix of agent, private dealer, gallery dealer, interior designer, curator, and traveling salesman, all thrown into one. But what they all have in common is that they sell art—sometimes a lot of it. And you've probably never heard of most of them. They don't advertise nationally; they don't have shows of artists' work; and they certainly don't go to gallery openings.

What they are doing is selling art to a variety of clients, such as hospitals, hotels, corporations, restaurants, resorts, and any other business or home that has bare walls and a suitable budget. They work with both corporate and private clients and usually handle a wide range of art styles.

Any artist who has worked with art consultants can tell you that many of them are demanding, pushy, persistent, and annoying. But the good ones are worth a thousand times over whatever fortitude it takes to deal with them. Finding the ones who are active is the secret to making money with them.

The best way to find active art consultants is by getting a tip from artists who know them firsthand. If you don't know any successful artists, think about attending an art expo and speaking with some of the exhibiting artists there, or even just researching trade publications such as the *Art in America Gallery Guide* or the *Artist's & Graphic Designer's Market*, a handy resource book that lists consultants under "art reps." Do as much research as possible before you contact the consultant; be sure she shows work of a similar price range and style to your own, and that she works professionally. If possible, visit her web site and look at her client list.

After you have assembled your list of appropriate art consultants, start contacting them. This should be a straightforward, but friendly, call: Introduce yourself and offer to send them work.

Listen carefully to their description of how they want to receive your work, and be sure to tailor your portfolio specifically to their requests. After sending out your packets, make sure to follow up within a week to confirm receipt. If they have not had a chance to review your work, schedule a time to call again. If they're interested, be prepared to ask them about commission splits, shipping, insurance, payment schedules, and discounts.

Will art consultants change your life? Maybe. Like my artist friend who suddenly looked so prosperous, you might also find your career revitalized by a talented art consultant. But finding an art consultant isn't easy. Before you can even go on the market for one, you need to make sure that you are prepared not just for the search but for the possibility of becoming a client. You need to have an updated portfolio and relevant pricing; you need to be steadily producing in case they receive a large commission. Successful art consultants place dozens of pieces of art a month, so they want artists who are energetic, if not driven, and who are capable of producing an extremely large amount of good work.

Many emerging artists find pricing especially tricky. If you are essentially an unknown artist, your prices should be reasonable, usually under $1,000. You can expect the art consultant to double your price when he presents it to the client, but you must also have a firm idea of what your bottom-line price is since art consultants are notorious for giving hefty discounts to their clients. Commissions vary anywhere from 10 percent to 60 percent; be sure to confirm the commission before signing on the dotted line.

As with galleries, finding the right art consultant who thinks you're the right artist is no small feat. Your work has to have broad appeal, your prices have to be competitive, and you must be well organized and professional when dealing with this little-known faction of the art world. But when you connect with the art consultants who respond to your work, the sales will happen. So start searching.

❧

Geoffrey Gorman, a former gallery director, attended the Maryland Institute of Art and the Boston Museum School. www.geoffreygormanart.com

SET DECORATORS

People who work with movie studios to create sets are called set decorators. Most set decorators belong to the Set Decorators Society of America/SDSA (www.setdecorators.org).

Once background sets are built, set decorators "dress" the set, creating an ambiance to complement the screenplay. Most productions require several sets and, thus. a variety of themes.

Set decorators are usually hired on a per-project basis, sometimes weekly or monthly. Some are contracted for a specific television series or motion picture. Their reputation is often word-of-mouth. They require a solid base of reliable vendor outlets.

They shop for artwork, décor, furniture, fabric, lighting and more. They mostly rent artwork but on occasion purchase it, often working with prop houses who maintain the artwork. Direct purchases of artwork may occur if a set is being utilized throughout an entire shooting season.

Prop houses generally rent items on a short-term basis, often providing door-to-door delivery services. Sometimes set decorators rent large quantities of items, receiving more than they actually need, so they have some leeway in their choices of usage on the set.

- Prop houses need "cleared" permission rights from the artist to rent artwork to set decorators.
- Most often the artist is not given a copyright mention during the credits.

An individual piece may rent for $150-250 per week, with price breaks for an extended time. A prop house would hope to make at least $3000 on the life of an art rental; thus, the artist is lucky to receive $1000 for the purchase and permission rights.

If rented, the set decorator splits the rental fee with the artist and sometimes assesses a percentage from that fee for marketing, advertising and sales generation. Rental fees can be 10-20% of the sales price.

PERMISSION REQUESTS

Before permission is signed, the artists will know:

- The title of the film or program, with a synopsis to determine the suitability
- An outline of the distribution of the film (TV, film festivals, public)
- How a specific artwork will be directly mentioned in a script

If permission is granted in writing to use or reproduce a specific work of art, the production company is legally obligated to provide a copyright credit line for the end credits.

If art is inadvertently used without permission, a retroactive license can be drawn up, as well as 10-40% additional charges for the use of an attorney.

Apparently, no reuse fee or royalty is paid for reruns or when motion pictures are turned into video or shown on TV. You would need to have that in your contract, but most likely the renter would not want to include it. Usually it is a flat fee; the longer used, the more you receive. If shown for less than two seconds, no licensing fees are paid but rental fees are. Major usage can bring $1000-5000.

Set decorators

Art Pic www.artpic2000.com

Art Tribe, Caroline Stover www.arttribe.net

Hand Prop Room www.jpr.com

Hollywood Studio Gallery, Ralph Foweler www.hollywoodstudiogallery.com

Mardine Davis www.mardinedavisart.com

Research online to find appropriate prop houses to approach with your artwork.

Educational TV

A noncommercial or educational broadcast company can use certain published works without the artist's consent. However, the station must pay the government-set royalty rate. If they don't volunteer this fee, it is considered an infringement, but they can use it without written permission by paying that fee to you. This usage can continue with the same piece for three years from the date of the first broadcast. Additional fees are required to be submitted at that time: for the second third-year period @ 50%. Each three-year period thereafter: 25%. Payment must be made July 31 of any given year that usage is made. The broadcast company must maintain the name and address of the copyright owner, the source from which the copyright piece was taken, a description or print-out of price, the title of program on which it was used and the date of the original broadcast.

If the broadcast company cannot find who the copyright owner is, they must set aside the required fee amount in a segregated trust fund for three years. If no one claims the royalties at that point, the funds can be recirculated. The amount set by a predetermined committee of law is between $20-120 for a variety of types of usage.

If you ever see your work on public TV without your permission, investigate it! You could have some money sitting in a trust account waiting for you.

PRIVATE COLLECTORS

Collectors are amazing. They can spend thousands of dollars within minutes.

Private buyers of artwork are as valuable a resource as a corporate art consultant. They can be a prime source for referrals to their many friends and business associates. You don't need to become their best friend, simply a business associate. This type of interaction could lead to huge benefits. You might be the only artist this collector buys from!

- Court private collectors: Invite them to a museum opening you plan to attend and give them a private tour.
- Imform them at least twice a year via mail or e-mail of one of your art events.
- Don't lose contact with them and, of course, with any artwork of yours they own.
- Treat them with the utmost honor and respect. If need be, spend some time educating them on art—specifically your art.

Over the years, your list of collectors will slowly grow. It will include not only all the people who have purchased from you, but all the people who have personally shown interest in your work.

Don't ever give the names of your private collectors to anyone—and don't expect another artist to give you his collectors' names. Don't even ask. The best way to associate with another artist's collectors would be to have a co-exhibit with that artist.

These collectors are your 20%—the 20% who bring in 80% of your annual income. They love your work. They can actually become your sales force, selling your work to their friends. They enjoy patronizing an artist, especially you, because you have shown them respect. Someday they might even allow you to use their homes for an exhibition.

Studio visit prep

Whether it be a private individual or gallery owner who comes to your studio, you need to be prepared.

- Limit the time of a studio visit for a private collector to no more than 30-45 minutes. If you overwhelm clients by showing them all your work, you will have tired people in front of you who don't want to buy anything, especially art. Let the patron lead the way. If he wants to stay longer than 30-45 minutes and it seems time profitably spent, allow it.
- Ask them what work of yours they are drawn to before they arrive—a particular style, originals or prints, a certain series. Have that ready to show.
- Anyone making the effort to visit your studio deserves your total focus. Do not allow interruptions. Even if she doesn't buy on the first visit, you will most likely see a purchase in the future.

Practice for a studio visit by showing your studio to a friend.

- Don't back out of your studio visit if you start getting stage fright. This fear goes away. It happens to Broadway performers and the like. Just go with it and overcome it.

Connect with the Buyer

Open Studios at Hunter's Point in San Francisco (where Open Studios originated) was a bit better than my highest expectations. I'd heard about it for years. Over 300 artists show their work, all within walking distance of each other. Parking is easy. The event even has a food bar. You can hang out all day (or even all weekend), meet friends, view art, chat with the artists, sit in the sun, and enjoy the fantastic views of the Bay. The place is bustling like an anthill all day.

Every studio I went into had a great presentation. All were clean and orderly and easy to navigate. About 50% of the artists had prices on their pieces (not enough for my needs). I think some of them thought they were a gallery venue and could get away without exposing prices. I don't know what their logic is.

I asked an artist the price of a triptych on the entryway wall. It was my favorite piece of those I had seen all day. She said, standing behind her protective desk with her husband by her side, "The price is on the painting." I went outside to search for the price but couldn't find it anywhere—not on the wall, not on the side (I failed to look on the bottom side of the piece)! I realized right then what a poor presentation this artist had given me. Here she has a potential client who is asking a price! She doesn't even escort me out to the piece, to tell me something about it, or about herself, or about her artwork in general. Such an opportunity down the drain! Not only that, but I can't find the price! Right action would be to take me out to the piece and chat with me. See how I react to the price. Ask me where I would be hanging it (as if I had already bought it). Tell me a story about when she was painting it, or what it means to her. Get me emotionally involved. Eventually tell me she can put a red dot on it and reserve it for me (not pressuring me to buy it). See how I react. If I say the price is too costly, she can lead me to another piece; after all, this is a triptych. Certainly if I have my eye on such a large piece and am asking the price, I must have a large house and a bit of money to spend. Perhaps she can split the triptych cost into three payments; will that make it easier for me? Perhaps she can deliver it to my house in her van, as it wouldn't fit in my car. There are so many options when someone asks the price of a piece, or asks a question about a piece. Don't let these types of opportunities escape you. Artists must be ready to start the emotional connection and the sale. To start a sale, emotional contact is essential. Ingrain the attitude, "All viewers are there to own a piece." Your attitude about selling will change. Choosing the right piece becomes the problem, not whether they will buy.

Chapter 9

Galleries

The gallery scene

The gallery search

Meeting with a gallery owner

Studio visits

Working with a gallery

Legalities

University galleries

Rental galleries

Co-op galleries

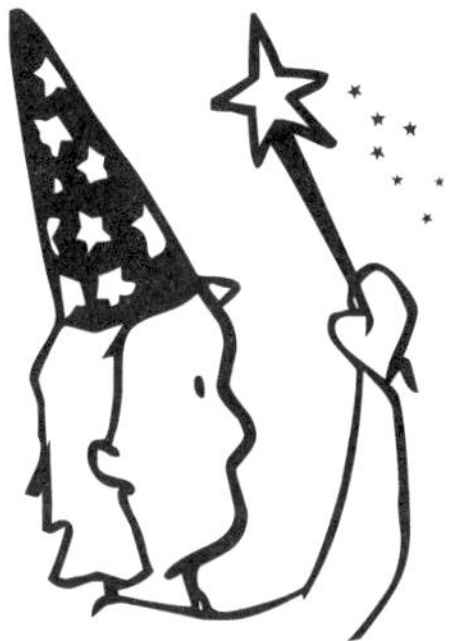

Only those who will risk going too far can possibly find out how far one can go. T S Eliot

The Gallery Scene

If you're an artist looking for a gallery to carry your work, you need to think creatively. What is it that will set your work apart from all the other artists searching for a gallery?

You might not realize how few people walk through any given gallery in one year. Do you know how many people who like art have never been in a gallery? Start asking and you'll be surprised. Most people find galleries overbearing, stiff and snobby and don't feel comfortable being in one, let alone looking at the art and considering buying. You're missing a huge hunk of the market if you think galleries are the only way to sell your work.

I advise artists to search for galleries in a reserved manner. They are generally listed last on any of my recommendations for venues in which to sell artwork. Unless you are the number-one person represented by the gallery, there are many drawbacks.

Artists often approach galleries before their time. Most art dealers and gallery directors want to represent artists who have already achieved critical recognition and have a substantial number of clients.

Respect

Galleries often don't seem to respect artists. Some pay them late, do not repair damaged artwork before returning it, and sometimes do not even return work. I cannot tell you the number of stories like this I have heard. Of course, there are some great gallery owners out there, too, but I've only heard a few stories about them.

A gallery can only promote a small number of artists at any given time. They want to promote artists whose work is the easiest to sell. If you don't fall into that category, they might just be storing your work rather than attempting to sell it.

One artist I know sells his pieces for up to $25,000. He does have a gallery affiliation—a very well-known gallery in New York City. I asked him why he stays with a gallery that neither sells his work nor gives him a show. He stated, "It sounds good to be listed with a gallery that has prestige, but I'd rather sell my own work because I make more money. I want the gallery around, though, for when I become famous and too busy to sell my own work. Then they will want to give me a show." This has worked for him because he can and does sell his own work (mostly in the five-digits).

Dealing with a gallery is a two-sided affair. You cannot abandon them and leave them totally to their own devices. They need to know you appreciate them.

Myths about galleries

- Galleries make or break an artist.
- You must be represented by a gallery to be a real artist.
- Gallery owners are good businesspeople.

Make a list of 20 local galleries to visit and review. When you visit the galleries, jot down all the information you can about each one. From your research, decide what gallery you want to be in. These are the ones you will be approaching.

Focus on galleries that have proven track records and carry work compatible with your own. When it comes down to the final choice, you want to know that the gallery is going to invest in your career. If you get the gallery to commit financially—buying work, framing, spending time on an exhibit, sending press releases—you know you have a good gallery. You can research galleries online at www.art-collecting.com/galleries.htm.

FACTORS TO INVESTIGATE

- Styles of art the gallery carries
- Price range and career status of the artists they represent. If they have very established artists selling for $15,000 and you are just beginning to approach galleries, you are probably barking up the wrong tree.
- Customer service you receive as a visitor to the gallery
- Mood, atmosphere, lighting
- Verify the reliability of the gallery through the Better Business Bureau, Chamber of Commerce or Artists Equity Association.
- Location, foot traffic

You're going to choose the gallery and sell yourself, your artwork and your story to them. When you know you've found the right gallery for your work, court them. Send them postcards of your openings, and attend their openings. It will take persistence—you've already verified that persistence pays off. Ideally, a gallery owner will have seen your work in local exhibits over the past years (remember, you sent postcards) and will know who you are.

When a gallery takes you on, they should give you a solo show within a year and buy at least one of your artworks. What are you there for, otherwise? They are investing in you!

INTRODUCTIONS

A good way to meet gallery owners is through charity balls or fundraising events. Gallery owners are bombarded by artists introducing themselves over the phone or in person. Show that you are involved in your community. Introducing yourself inconspicuously can be the best path to becoming acquainted with a gallery owner or museum curator.

Most gallery owners get a lot of e-mails; many don't have time to review them. Most gallery owners will not review a CD that is sent unsolicited unless they see an

THE GALLERY SEARCH

Know what your artwork's most unique quality is and flaunt it.

Your goal in sending a portfolio to a gallery is to get the director to your studio to view your artwork.

example of your work that really intrigues them on the cover—they just don't have time. If you are going to mail something, send them a few printed reproductions (or four to six on a standard-size sheet of paper). They can review it quickly and then proceed to your well-designed web site, which is, of course, noted on your letterhead.

Add all galleries that interest you to your mailing list. You will, ultimately, send a postcard inviting them to your openings. Over time they will come to recognize your style and perhaps go online to view your web site and even come to an opening. Oftentimes, they already have enough artists to rep. Eventually, though, they might need to add a new artist to their stable.

Reference sources

Art in America Annual Guide www.artinamericamagazine.com
This directory lists galleries, consultants, museum curators and other art world professionals. It can be found on most magazine stands in the summer months.

Art Now Gallery Guides
Found in most areas of the country, free, at galleries

Collectors Guide to Art of New Mexico www.collectorsguide.com
A beautiful publication listing galleries and artists in New Mexico

TOP 10 REASONS WHY GALLERIES REJECT ARTISTS (IT'S NOT WHAT YOU THINK)

by Sylvia White

Most artists harbor the fantasy that if they could only find one art dealer who loved and believed in their work, their career would be set. They secretly believe that there exists a special person who can catapult them to fame. Many artists spend most of their careers searching for "the perfect gallery." And, like all quests towards perfection, it is neverending. If they already have a gallery, it's not good enough; if they are looking for their first gallery, they dream about the moment when someone sets eyes on their work and offers them a solo show immediately. The harsh reality is that having a gallery love your work is only one very small part of what goes into the decision to represent an artist. From a gallery's point of view, adding an artist to their stable is much like adding a stock to one's portfolio. There are many complicated factors to take into consideration, and liking the "stock" usually has very little to do with the decision. There is no doubt that while liking the artist's work is certainly the first criterion, there are several other hurdles that must be overcome before a gallery will commit to an artist. Understanding those hurdles will help you to present your work effectively to galleries and detach yourself from the inevitable sense of personal failure that follows when a gallery rejects your artwork.

Too similar

A gallery looks at the group of artists they represent much like an artist looks at a painting. It is not so much the individual artist who is considered, but, rather, how the art fits into the existing group. Often galleries are reluctant to take artists who are too similar to an artist they already represent.

Too different

All galleries try to create a niche for themselves by representing artists who are stylistically similar and would appeal to their core group of collectors. If your work is outside the arbitrary parameters they have established, you are out of luck.

Too far away

Unless you have already established a reputation elsewhere, galleries are reluctant to work with artists outside their regional area. Issues surrounding shipping costs and the inconvenience of getting and returning work in an expedient manner often make it not worth it.

Too fragile/difficult to store

Regardless of how big a gallery is, there is never enough storage space. Galleries shy away from work that is three-dimensional, easily breakable, heavy or hard to handle.

Too expensive

Most artists undervalue their work. But, occasionally I will come across an artist with a totally unrealistic sense of how to price his work. Prices are established by the law of supply and demand. If a gallery feels they cannot price your work fairly and still make a 50% commission, they will not be willing to take a chance on you.

Too cheap

Artists who only do works on paper (photographers, etc) often cannot generate enough income from sales to make an exhibition worth it to a gallery. If you have 20 pieces in a show and each piece sells for $500 and your show completely sells out, your gallery has only made $5000, barely enough to cover the costs of the postage, announcement and opening reception.

Too difficult

Entering into a relationship with a gallery is, in many ways, similar to entering into a marriage. It's a relationship that needs to be able to endure candid dialog about the things that are often the most difficult to discuss with anyone—your artwork and money. Both the artist and the gallery need to have a level of trust and comfort that will guarantee honest communication. If a gallery perceives you as being a difficult person to work with, they tend to veer away.

Too inexperienced

Many artists start approaching galleries too soon, before their work has fully matured. Most critics and curators say it takes an artist several years after college for their work to develop fully stylistically. Galleries want to make sure that once they commit to you, your work will not make radical and/or unpredictable changes. Even if a gallery loves your work, they may want to watch your development over a period of years to confirm their initial opinion. Artists must also have enough work of a similar sensibility to mount an exhibition.

Too experienced

The gallery's fear of failure is strong, particularly in this economic climate. Careful to be sensitive to a price point that is right for their audience, galleries may not be financially able to risk representing artists who are farther along in their career, therefore demanding higher prices, than emerging younger artists. Artists with a long sales history of gradually appreciating prices may find themselves priced out of the current market.

❧

Sylvia White has been working with artists for over 25 years. Her company—Contemporary Artists' Services—is located in Los Angeles. Consultations can be arranged in person, by phone or by e-mail. www.artadvice.com info@artadvice.com

APPROACHING A GALLERY

Offer the owner with whom you've received a meeting something unique—in quality, style of work and presentation.

- State briefly in your cover letter why you think the gallery is the right place for your work. Did you see an exhibit? Did someone refer you? Follow up with a call to see what the gallery owner thought of your portfolio, and, hopefully, to arrange for a studio visit.
- Don't ask for a show or suggest that the gallery represent you. Suggest they come to your studio to view your work, even if you live out of town. If you are from out of town, let them know when you will be in their area to bring some of your pieces to them.
- Enclose a SASE for convenient return of your portfolio. Gallery owners don't like to pay.
- Give gallery owners four weeks to review your work and get back to you. If, by that time, they have not called or returned your portfolio in the provided SASE, call them, but don't be pushy.

MEETING AT THE GALLERY

If and when you finally do get a meeting, go prepared:

- Confirm your appointment the day before.
- Arrive 10 minutes early so you can relax.
- Don't show your work to a subordinate of the gallery owner or director. This is a waste of time.
- Don't play the part of the desperate, struggling artist.Take the attitude that you are interviewing the gallery. Do you want to work with them?

Make notes after your meeting: general feeling about the gallery, quality of artwork the gallery carries, price range and subject matters, general impression of the exterior of the gallery, foot traffic, how long the gallery has been in business, quality and types of shops nearby.

ITEMS TO BRING

- Portfolio, original reviews, exhibit announcements, retail price list
- Several original pieces of your work (if not too burdensome). You should be ready to leave these with the gallery owner on consignment. If you do leave any pieces, you must get a signed receipt stating the retail price to the collector, the gallery's commission, and the condition in which work was received in the form of a "consignment agreement." Add to your original consignment agreement

MEETING WITH A GALLERY OWNER

Assist your gallery; give them ideas for marketing your art.

A consignment agreement states that art shall be held in trust for the artist's benefit and will not be subject to any claim by creditors.

as necessary when you bring in new artworks and take away (or sell) others. A consignment agreement should list the title, medium, size, overall description, perhaps a photo, date placed at gallery, name and signature of gallery owner, as well as your name and signature. (Download a consignment agreement at www.artmarketing.com/downloads.html.)

Ask these questions when a gallery shows interest

How long has the gallery been in business?

Who has shown in the gallery in the past? Do you handle PR for openings?

Who pays for invitations for openings? Refreshments?

When will the work be selected for the show? When will the reception be?

Will your show be advertised?

Do you have insurance for theft, fire, flood, and handling damages?

Who pays for framing, shipping? When will the gallery need the artwork?

What date will the show be hung? How long will the show hang?

How do you pay your artists?

One artist in Florida had his work at a gallery that closed its doors suddenly due to bankruptcy, not even informing its artists of the situation. The police came in, claimed all the goods (finding no consignment agreements) and eventually auctioned off the artwork. A restaurant purchased the entire collection of one artist for quite a small sum. The artist didn't know about any of this as he wasn't doing his part and keeping in contact with the gallery. One day he walked into the restaurant and saw all his paintings on the wall. He was quite excited—a big sale! He called his gallery only to find that they had closed due to bankruptcy. The only way he could recover his work was if he could prove that he had a consignment agreement—which he hadn't bothered to procure. He never got a cent for his pieces.

UNDERSTANDING GALLERIES

After talking to several galleries that have been in business for some time, I tried to figure out how much income they need and how much in expenses they incur. By looking at the theoretical calculations below, you, as an artist, will be able to understand more clearly why a gallery needs to receive a 50% commission on its sales. You will understand also why its salespeople must be able to sell a certain number of paintings each month, just like a car dealer, in order to make ends meet. If an artist's work is not selling, then the gallery owner must find another artist's work that will sell. It's that simple.

The following hypothetical gallery has six artists. All of them make a full-time living at creating their artwork. In this scenario, the gallery owner earns the same wage as the best-paid artist. The other salespeople are making the same wages as the five other artists. The gallery makes a profit of 4% of total sales.

Gallery income

Artist receives $75,000. This artist is more popular than the rest; thus, he creates and sells more than the other five. His retail price on a painting averages $5000. He produces and sells 30 paintings each year.

The gallery receives 50%	$ 75,000
Five artists sell 10 paintings @ an average of $2000. Each artist makes $50,000 per year (50x$2000@50%x5)	250,000
Two part-time salespersons @ $25,000	(50,000)
One full-time salesperson at $50,000	(50,000)
Owner's salary at $75,000	(75,000)
Gallery expenses at $11,000 per month: rent $5000, employee taxes and IRA $2000, advertising $1000, supplies/computer $1000, utilities/misc./interest/openings $2000	(132,000)
Profit of 4% of total sales	$18,000

STUDIO VISITS

The business relationship between gallery and artist must be based on mutual respect and trust. If this is not the basis, you can count on it failing.

If a gallery is interested in your work, the director will probably want to visit your studio. Having the gallery owner make a studio visit is better than bringing your work to the gallery. He is now making the effort to come to you and see *all* your work, your history, your story—who you are and what you create—a big coup for you. Don't expect that she will buy a piece or sign a contract with you immediately. Plan this visit to be at least an hour, though it might only last 15 minutes.

Know what you want to say and create a clear outline. You don't have to memorize anything; just have an idea.

Take notice of what they are asking—there is a reason. Are they interested more in your philosophy or your technique? Are they concerned about the lack of press releases you have framed on the wall?

- Give simple, clear directions to your studio. If you live in the wilderness, ask them to call you from a nearby, easy-to-find landmark, meet them there, and escort them to your studio.
- Have a tidy studio. You want them to see your work and you, not the dust and clutter you haven't cleaned for months.
- Have some refreshments available.
- Hang your best work in prominent positions. If there is anything you don't want them to see, take it completely out of the studio.
- Allow the gallery owner to conduct the interview. You are not selling at this time; you are simply showing.
- Be prepared for questions such as: your major influences, sources of imagery, medium.
- Don't answer the phone while you have someone in your studio.

Acceptance/rejection

If, ultimately, you are not accepted at this time, ask them for referrals. What do you have to lose? Gallery owners around town have lots of information on other gallery situations. They might send you to just the right spot, or tell you that you're not ready and why.

Should you be rejected, send a card of appreciation for their time. Maybe a handmade card will grab them and encourage them to rethink their decision. Be different from the other artists who just take "no" sitting down. Show them you are still interested. Keep mailing them invitations to your openings.

When your art is accepted by a gallery, your job is not over. You have to stay on top of the gallery to keep them promoting you. One gallery or one show isn't going to make your career. A career is built upon a series of exhibitions, sales, awards, and commissions.

Usually you will not be accepted into a gallery at the first meeting; in fact, be suspicious if that happens. Galleries need time to share their ideas with sales personnel as well as think over your work.

What a gallery owner really wants besides your art is assurance that you will not be a "flake." He wants to work with an artist who is reliable, considerate, respectful, who continues to produce a body of work and is honest. Of course, the artist wishes the same from her gallery!

If you haven't noticed by now, it's a long road to winning over a gallery owner. Be patient. Many artists finally get into a well-known gallery after 20 years of "emerging."

Studio sales

If a collector sees your work at the gallery you're associated with and traces you to your studio in order to get a reduced rate, this collector will be sadly disappointed.

- Never undersell the gallery; sell at the same price.
- Since you know they found you via the gallery, you will be giving the gallery their commission. Can you imagine the gallery owner's surprise when this happens unbeknownst to him and you send the gallery a $1500 check? Maybe they'll treat you with more respect!
- Make it clear in your gallery contract that it is legal for you to make sales from your studio. You have clients you have dealt with personally for years, and you still want to service their needs. If a gallery can't understand that, they are simply greedy.

Question

The son of a former client of mine recently became represented by a gallery and is having some success. He has been commissioned to do a painting by a designer who saw his work in the gallery. His gallery expects to receive a 50% commission even though the gallery has done nothing towards this new business except to have his paintings on the walls. What should the commission be?

Answer

The gallery *did* do something to bring the commission! They made his work available to the public. Working with a gallery is a two-way deal. If you consider the gallery an angel in disguise, you will be much better off. Would this young artist have received any commission without the gallery showing his work? Probably not.

WORKING WITH A GALLERY

A dealer should not have a stable of artists; an artist should have a stable of dealers. Mark Kostabi

LEGALITIES

The most common way an artist becomes known by a gallery is through the recommendation of a friend.

Contracts

Even if you get accepted into a gallery, it doesn't mean you're going to have a solo show or any type of show. If it's not in your contract, don't count on it. Artists call me very excited about their acceptance into a gallery, only to find out that they won't be receiving a solo show. Some owners get greedy and don't want the gallery down the block to show your work—so they sign you up without guaranteeing anything just to keep you out of the marketplace. Make sure you have a contract you understand and like.

Even if you are having only one show at the gallery and you are not being officially represented, you need a contract. Many gallery owners don't want to sign contracts. But you do! Don't ever agree to show your work at a gallery without a contract. You are a businessperson who knows your rights. Have a contract ready.

Commissions

So you've found the right gallery, but they want 50% of the sales? Wow! You didn't know they took that much. Remember the cost of the Open Studio you put on? Or that group show you held? Generally, a gallery owner has even more costs due to higher rent and upscale clientele. If you cringe at a 50% commission, don't even approach a gallery.

- The commission arrangement in your gallery agreement should be tailored to your particular situation. If the cost of materials for your work is quite high, you would want it to state that the materials, installation and foundry fees are deducted before the gallery's commission.
- If you provide framed work, you want to make sure you get paid for the frames.
- An approach some galleries use is a sliding scale commission: works under $3000 are 50/50; for works $3000-8000, the gallery gets 40%; for works over $8000, the gallery gets 30%.

Tip

- Don't forget to discuss and state in your contract with a gallery (or consultant) how much they can negotiate down on any of your retail prices. Sometimes they need this for leverage, so let them have it.

ARTIST-GALLERY AGREEMENT

This is an Agreement between ("Artist") ______________________, residing at ___________________________,
and ("Gallery") ___________, at ____.

The terms of this Agreement are as follows:

1. **Limited, Exclusive Agency.** Artist hereby appoints Gallery his exclusive/non-exclusive agent for the sale and exhibition of his works of art in the following geographical area:______________________________. The Gallery shall have the right of first selection of works produced by Artist for inclusion in the show(s) which it will present. Any works not selected by the Gallery may be sold by the Artist.

2. **Creation, Title and Receipt.** Artist hereby warrants that he created and possessed unencumbered title to, and Gallery acknowledges receipt of, the works of art on the attached Consignment Schedule ("Schedule").

3. **Sales.** Sales shall be made at a price not less than the price ("Retail $") on Schedule, which doesn't include sales tax or delivery costs. The Gallery will supply the Artist with its signed resale certificate and its resale number for Artist's records. Gallery shall receive ____% commission on the sales price on sales made by Gallery; ____ % of the sales price on sales made directly by the Artist; ____ % of the rental fees on rentals arranged by the Gallery; ____ % of the amount received for prizes and awards granted to the Artist when such prizes and awards are obtained for the Artist by the Gallery; ____ % of lecture fees for lectures arranged for the Artist by the Gallery. The Gallery may give a trade discount, which shall not exceed ____% of sales price without the Artist's written consent on sales to museums, galleries, decorators and architects. In the case of such discount sales, the amount of the discount shall be deducted from the Gallery's sales commission. The Gallery shall use its best efforts to promote the sale of the Artist's consigned works, to support a market for the Artist's work, and to provide continuous sales representation in the following manner: ____
____.

4. **Payment on Gallery's Sales.** On outright sales: Gallery shall pay Artist the balance of sales price after its commission within thirty (30) days of purchaser's payment to Gallery. If purchaser pays in installments, all monies received by Gallery from purchaser shall be distributed pro rata to Artist and Gallery in accordance with their respective percentage shares of the total sale price, and Artist's share shall be paid within thirty (30) days of Gallery's receipt of any installment payment until Artist's share is paid in full. It is expressly agreed that any default of a purchaser from Gallery shall be borne solely by Gallery and Gallery shall, notwithstanding such default, pay Artist his percentage share of sales price within one hundred eighty (180) days of any such sale on installment terms.

5. **Payment on Artist's Sales.** The Gallery shall receive _____ % of any sales made by the Artist personally, without the assistance of the Gallery, provided, however, that no commission shall be paid on any sales referred to in this paragraph, unless the Gallery makes sales in the contract year of at least $ ______ for the Artist. Artist shall pay Gallery its commission within thirty (30) days of the purchaser's payment to Artist. If purchaser pays in installments, Artist shall pay Gallery its percentage share of each payment by purchaser to Artist within thirty (30) days of Artist's receipt of any installment payments.

6. **Commissions.** Gallery shall be entitled to receive _____ % of the price of any commissions given to Artist to create works of art when such commissions are obtained for him by Gallery, and _____ % of any such commissions Artist procures during the term of this Agreement.

7. **Exhibitions.** During the term of this agreement, Gallery shall hold at least __ solo exhibition(s) every ____ months for Artist and shall use its best efforts to arrange other solo exhibition(s) for Artist and for the inclusion of Artist's work in group exhibitions in other galleries or museums, provided, however, that Artist's work may not be included in any group exhibition without his prior written consent. Failure to do so shall entitle Artist to terminate this Agreement upon thirty (30) days' written notice to Gallery. Although the Gallery may arrange for representation of the Artist by another agency with the Artist's written consent, the Gallery shall pay such agency by splitting its own commission. When the Artist has a one-man show at the Gallery, all related costs will be borne by the Gallery for such exhibition; including, but not limited to, advertising, printing, reception, framing, packing and freight. Should the Gallery lend out for approval to a client a piece of Artwork by said Artist, the Gallery will be responsible for Artist's commission if work is stolen, lost or damaged, just as in a sale. Should the piece not be returned within seven days, it will be considered sold and Artist will expect his commission in due time as provided in this contract. Should the Artist give the Gallery his mailing list to use for any exhibit, the Gallery shall respect confidentiality of same and only use it for the Artist's personal show. After the exhibition, frames, photographs, negatives and any other tangible property created in the course of the exhibition shall be the property of the Artist. The _________ shall bear the cost of shipping the works to the Gallery. The ________ shall bear the cost of framing. The Gallery shall bear all other costs incident upon the show. The Artist shall be free to exhibit and sell any work not consigned to the Gallery under this Agreement.

8. **Rented Artwork.** A Rental Agreement must be signed by interested party and Artist.
9. **Statements of Account.** Gallery shall give Artist a Statement of Account within fifteen (15) days after the end of each calendar quarter. The Statement shall detail Artist's works sold/rented/leased during the calendar quarter (to include at least price, date, name and address of purchaser, payments made to Artist, payments owed Artist on installment purchases, and location of any unsold work not located at Gallery.
10. **Reproduction Rights.** Artist hereby reserves the right to copy, photograph or reproduce each work of art consigned to Gallery. Gallery agrees that it will not permit any of the works of art to be copied, photographed or reproduced except for the purpose of appearing in a catalog or advertisement without the prior written consent of Artist and will state, "The right to copy, photograph or reproduce the work(s) of art identified herein is reserved by the Artist." Notwithstanding the foregoing, reproduction rights may be specifically sold by Gallery with the Artist's prior written consent. Gallery shall not receive any commissions on royalties or licensing of reproduction rights unless sold or arranged by Gallery, in which case Gallery's commission shall be ________%. Artist is free to procure publisher at own time and expense. Gallery will receive no commissions on these procurements.
11. **Insurance.** Gallery will provide all-risk insurance on Artist's works of art listed on the Schedule of up to ____% of retail price.
12. **Termination of Agreement.** This Agreement shall terminate on _______________. Upon termination, Gallery shall return within thirty (30) days all Artist's works of art which are held on consignment.
13. **Return of Works.** All costs of return (including packing, transportation and insurance) shall be paid as follows: ___% by the Artist, ____% by the Gallery. The Gallery may return any consigned work on thirty (30) days' written notice. The Artist may withdraw his consigned work on thirty (30) days' written notice. If the Artist fails to accept return of the works within ___ days after written request by the Gallery, the Artist shall pay reasonable storage costs. The Gallery agrees to return consigned works in the same good condition as received.
14. **Loss or Damage.** The Gallery shall not intentionally commit or authorize any physical defacement, mutilation, alteration, or destruction of any of the consigned works. The Gallery shall be responsible for the proper cleaning, maintenance, and protection of consigned work, and shall also be responsible for the loss or damage of consigned work, whether the work be on the Gallery's premises, on loan, on approval, on rental/lease or otherwise removed from its premises.
15. **Maintenance.** If restoration is undertaken for any consigned work, all repairs and restoration shall have the Artist's written permission. The Artist shall be consulted as to his recommendations with regard to all such repairs and restoration, and will be given first opportunity to accomplish said repairs and restoration for a reasonable fee.
16. **Miscellaneous.** This Agreement may not be assigned by Gallery without Artist's prior written consent. This Agreement constitutes the entire understanding between the parties. Its terms cannot be modified except by an instrument in writing signed by the parties involved. A waiver of any breach of any of the provisions of this Agreement shall not be construed as a continuing waiver of other breaches of the same or other provisions hereof.
17. **Arbitration.** All disputes arising out of this Agreement shall be submitted to final and binding arbitration. The arbitrator shall be selected in accordance with the rules of Arbitration and Mediation Services. If such service is not available, the dispute shall be submitted to arbitration in accordance with the laws of _________. The arbitrator's decision shall be final, and judgment may be entered upon it by any court having jurisdiction thereof.
18. **Severability.** If any part of this Agreement is held to be illegal, void or unenforceable for any reason, such holding shall not affect the validity and enforceability of any other part.
19. **Moral Right.** The Gallery will not permit any use of the Artist's name or misuse of the consigned works which would reflect discredit on his reputation as an artist or which would violate the spirit of the work.
20. **Security.** The consigned works shall be held in trust for the benefit of the Artist, and shall not be subject to claim by a creditor of the Gallery. In the event of any default by the Gallery, the Artist shall have all the rights of a secured party under the Uniform Commercial Code.

21. **Governing Law.** This agreement shall be governed by the laws of the State of ______.

ARTIST ____ DATE______

GALLERY OWNER/AGENT ____ DATE______

FROM A GALLERY OWNER'S PERSPECTIVE

by Jason Horejs

Step into my head for a moment to better understand what a gallery owner is thinking as he looks at your work. I am asking myself four questions as I review an artist's work.

1. Do I like the work? This is a visceral reaction. If I think the work is cool and unique and am excited by it, I will probably be able to create a similar excitement in my collectors. If, on the other hand, the work does nothing for me, it matters not how famous the artist is, nor how trendy the style; I'm not going to be able to get behind the work and sell it.
2. Will the work appeal to my collectors, and will they buy it as priced? I can't answer these questions with absolute certainty, but having been in the gallery business for half my life, I can be right more times than not.
3. Do I like the artist? Life is too short and there are too many good artists out there for me to represent an artist who is difficult or disorganized. I am looking for artists with whom I can build long-term relationships, who are friendly, and on top of their game.
4. Is there a niche for this artist in my gallery? Does the work feel like it will fit? Is it too close in style or substance to other artists I carry? Will it fill a niche for price, subject, or size?

The gallery owner briefly directs his attention to your work and formulates a judgment that could have lasting repercussions for the gallery.

While each gallery asks a different set of questions, the substance is uniform: "How much have you sold?" "Are you seriously pursuing your work?" "If your work sells well, will you be able to replace it?" "How much work have you created in the last year?" "How many galleries represent you?" "What is your background?"

Answer the questions honestly, composing your responses to show yourself in a professional light. Consider, for example, the question: "How much work have you sold in the last year?" Perhaps you have not sold much in the last year. Nevertheless, do not respond by saying, "I'm afraid sales have been slow for me the past year," nor by deprecating yourself with flimsy excuses. Keep your response positive and concise: "In the last year I have increased my sales by 50% and can no longer spend my time in marketing my work. Frankly, I need to be in the studio painting."

While you did not answer the question precisely, you did let the owner know you are increasing sales, and that you need the gallery to do the marketing you are now too busy to do.

Don't mistake a question for an opportunity to ramble on for an hour; answer and get on with it. Time is of the essence.

❧

This excerpt is from Chapter 13 of *"STARVING" TO SUCCESSFUL*, published in 2009 by Jason Horejs who owns a gallery in Scottsdale, AZ. His book can be purchased online at www.xanadugallery.com. He does consulting with artists and has also created a software program to keep better records of inventory, sales and collectors called *ART TRACKER*.

UNIVERSITY GALLERIES

Never bring your artwork or portfolio to an opening; that would be too intrusive.

Many artists overlook the local college or university gallery scene, thinking it's only for students and alumni. University galleries usually show a variety of styles from a sampling of artists. I've known artists receiving five-digit figures for their pieces sold through university galleries.

College exhibition spaces (and small college museums) are attempting to enhance their educational mission and provide a cultural program for the surrounding community as well as their students. University galleries are often open to avant-garde and installation work.

- On occasion they pay a stipend to "borrow" your work (and, of course, pay for its transport and hanging).
- Sometimes they want the exhibiting artist to provide a lecture for interested patrons.

For many patrons, a university gallery is a more congenial atmosphere than the sterile, commercial gallery.

Tips

- Explore university galleries in your community.
- Keep your eye on the "Calls for Exhibits" posted in various art newspapers.
- Attend some of your local college gallery openings. Be sure to introduce yourself to the director; many times they have group shows and your work might be appropriate for a particular show. They need to know you and your art. A university exhibition space becomes a networking tool for artists who take advantage of it.

Museum rental galleries

Many museums across the nation have a division that rents (and sometimes sells) works of emerging artists. Some smaller art centers do the same. Check out your local area to see if there is a rental or sales program you can join. If they don't have one, become an advocate and help start one!

Allen Memorial Art Museum, OH www2.oberlin.edu/amam/artrent.html

Portland Art Museum www.portlandartmuseum.org
Over 2000 original works in various media by local artists

MOMA/San Francisco www.sfmoma.org/museumstore/artists_overview.htm
A busy venue for renting or buying

Los Angeles County Museum of Art www.lacma.org/shop/arsg.aspx

SAM Gallery www.seattleartmuseum.org/Visit/visitRSG.asp

Your studio

Use your studio as a rental gallery for private individuals as well as businesses. Giving these people the option of a lease will open doors to more sales. Use a legal agreement if you go this route. (Download a lease agreement at www.artmarketing.com/downloads.html.)

RENTAL GALLERIES

You will find many advertisements, especially in major cities, for gallery space to rent. The only time you want to rent space to exhibit is when you have a large customer base in a particular area and need an exhibition venue. When you rent such a space, you become responsible for all the work: invitations, PR and sales.

Many years ago, I operated a rental gallery in a close-knit, small community I lived in. It was loved (and honored—no one ever damaged a piece) by both the artists and lessees. For most leasers, it was their introduction to "live" art; most often they could not afford to purchase a piece, although we did sell a few pieces in the couple of years the gallery functioned. They loved, however, having original pieces on their walls.

CO-OP GALLERIES

Co-op galleries are well-respected and have been around for years.

An artist-run gallery, sometimes called a co-op gallery, is an exhibition space run by a group of artists. Artists share costs of rent, sales staff and opening costs. Co-op galleries can be a perfect exhibition venue for an emerging artist. Most co-op galleries require monthly dues and a commitment to sit and sell for a period of time each month. Often, you can join a cooperative gallery even if you don't live in the area.

Strength in numbers

Opening a gallery as an individual artist is too large a task, so a cooperative gallery—even just four artists working together—could create a great venue for sales. Hopefully, you will form a group of like-minded artists who want to expand their career and will be willing to spend time brain-storming innovative sales possibilities; for example, sponsoring talks at your co-op gallery on beginning a collection could bring in new clients.

Faults with co-op galleries

- Display of work is often chaotic; too many pieces are hanging too close together. The presentation is haphazard—too many fingers in the pie. Hiring a manager, director or curator could be worth the cost to bring the quality up a notch.
- Salesmanship is often nonexistent. Gallery "sitters" are often not familiar with the artists in the gallery, where the price list is and other aspects. This unfamiliarity can be disheartening when you're a customer.

Artist-run galleries

Art/Not Terminal, Seattle, WA www.antgallery.org

Atlantic Gallery, New York, NY www.atlanticgallery.org

Artists Space, New York, NY www.artistsspace.org

Bromfield Art Gallery, Boston, MA www.bromfieldgallery.com

Chicago Artists' Coalition www.chicagoartistscoalition.org/coalition-gallery/

Pleiades Gallery, New York, NY www.pleiadesgallery.com

Ward-Nasse Gallery, New York, NY www.wardnasse.org

Woman Made Gallery, Chicago, IL www.womanmade.org

Don't forget about local community centers that have a small gallery space and often sponsor openings. It's a great way to initiate your career or to take it to a new level.

Tip

- If you aren't part of a cooperative gallery, at least attempt to get a few artist-friends together to brainstorm monthly. Psychologically, it can be a big help to see others' perspectives.
- Create an event with a group of three other artists, alternating homes for a quarterly weekend sale.

Chapter 10

Art Placement in Businesses

The corporate market

Healthcare settings

Hotels

Wineries

Religious organizations

Small businesses

Interior designers

Architects

Real estate

Publishing and licensing

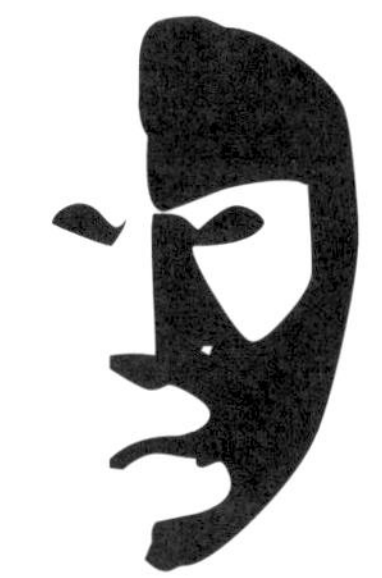

We should not let our fears hold us back from pursuing our hopes.

John F Kennedy

THE CORPORATE MARKET

Many corporations consider their support of the arts to be part of their public relations. They are not necessarily measuring their return on the dollar.

Corporations have been collecting art for a long time. Art is not always a decorative item for corporations; it can mean an investment, prestige, reputation or a tool used to help define a corporation's brand. Many industry giants are very competitive, and it is necessary to project a forward-thinking, progressive image. Art can do that.

Many times a corporation will have an in-house manager for their art collection. Sometimes this person is assisted by an independent art consultant who helps with purchase choices and curates the collection. Some companies use a committee instead of an individual to curate a collection.

Some companies send their art collection on tour, promoting their brand and reputation. Some publish catalogs of their collection. Some display it throughout their campus and allow tours open to the public. Some companies sponsor art talks open to the public.

Two great corporate art collections

Microsoft (WA) www.microsoft.com/mscorp/artcollection artevent@microsoft.com Reservations are a must; guided tours only. Sol LeWitt, Ursula Von Rydingsvard, Chuck Close and more.

Pepsi (NY) www.sirpepsi.com Open daylight hours, free, no reservations needed. Outdoor sculpture by Calder, Dubuffet, Ernst, Laurens, Lipshitz, Lipton, Moore, Oldenburg, Smith, Giocometti and more.

Researching corporations

It is good to understand what the aim of a corporate collection is before approaching them with your artwork. Be sure it is clear to you why you feel your work would make a good fit with the corporate collection already in place.

- Seeking out this business market takes some talent and creativity, but the rewards can be high.
- Don't think only big corporations buy art; small companies do too.
- To receive a commission from a corporation, you don't necessarily have to be well known.

Keep your eyes open when you are out and about. Does your doctor have a beautiful office but absolutely no artwork? When you see this, either take immediate action and find the CEO of the company, or make a note to call him and try to set up an appointment to show your portfolio. If the person seems hesitant and has many excuses due to budget, bring in your idea about leasing (see page 49).

Subscribe to your local paper (yes, it can be a business deduction). Search the business section for leads. Is a company constucting a new building, moving to a new location, getting a new CEO? Be creative and think of an excuse to approach them. Is an interior design firm redecorating an old wing of the hospital? Keep your ears and eyes open.

Banks and institutions sometimes have unused wall space. Approach them with the idea of selling a series of local scenes—originals or prints. Be sure to offer their employees some kind of deal as well. If buying is not on their agenda, try to procure an exhibit.

Let's not forget other public places: designer salons, automobile showrooms, hotels, restaurants and even sports arenas. These venues have finally become acceptable for professional artists as places to exhibit their work. Why? Because they expose the work, and, thus, it sells!

When meeting about this type of potential exhibition space and proposing an exhibition, have a contract that includes:

- who will pay for insurance
- who will pay mailing and printing of show invitations
- who is responsible for sales; can you post your phone number or web site?
- who is responsible for hanging and lighting

Especially in smaller, closer-knit communities, think of this preliminary research as the beginning work to forge networking contacts and future sales or leases. One good sale almost inevitably leads to another. Remember that you are in this business for the long haul.

Tips

- When making a cold call to a corporation, ask for the Purchasing Department. Then ask for the person in charge of buying art or furnishings. Tell him you are an artist and would like to show him your portfolio. Again, if he is hesitant, mention your lease program or your reasonably priced prints. Remember, it's common to get the runaround. Don't give up; don't let the ball drop.
- If you have prints and giclées that you can offer them at a lower price than your originals, you are ahead of the game. Start small with prints and work up to selling an original piece.
- Many people are not experienced in buying art. They have heard horror stories. Most people think that art is an "investment." Not true (as you know). Art is something to be enjoyed in the moment. Reenforce the idea of buying locally.
- As a last resort, ask them if they have fundraisers. If so, create a proposal (see pages 76-80).

Be clear on how you handle commissions. If you don't like being directed by a client, don't do them—you'll only get into trouble. (See Chapter 11.)

Working with an art consultant is one of the best ways to connect to larger corporations.

- Perhaps a busy doctor's office might allow you to hang one of your prints. Make sure you to can put a little blurb about the cost, how to contact you, and your web site.
- When you do get an appointment at a large corporation, don't make it a burden for the person you are meeting. She is busy with many other obligations. Come organized and businesslike. Bring 10-20 8x10" photo prints. If you have one, small, easy-to-carry sample of your work, you could also bring that. Be sure to bring something to leave with the person; one of the 8x10" photo prints is perfect. If he likes your work at all, he will hang it. When people see your piece in his office, it will reignite his interest in having "live art" in the halls. Keep him on your mailing list. Invite him to any shows you are having, local or distant. Let him know politely and in an unintrusive manner that you still want to do business (and that you are still in business)!
- Being part of the local Chamber of Commerce will introduce you to business owners.
- Develop an effective sales script for the telephone to get a meeting. Study *Selling Art 101* for great ideas on scripting your calls.
- Create a dynamic presentation specifically for the person(s) you'll be meeting. Think about what objections might arise, and try to be knowledgeable about overcoming them.
- Follow up with a personal invitation to have a studio visit.
- Have a lease program in place for potential follow-up.
- Keep track of all your telephone conversations and meetings with businesses. Be on top of it. (Download a client status record at www.artmarketing.com/downloads.html.)

Corporations can aid an artist in several ways

- Selling work in a corporate gallery
- Purchasing works directly from an artist
- Leasing artwork
- Having a grant program

HEALTHCARE SETTINGS

With an aging population and ongoing technology growth, the healthcare arena is a booming sector. Art appears in most facilities, in the form of prints or originals, giving a vibrant feel to a medical center. A trend to humanize hospitals, doctors' offices, clinics, outpatient facilities, senior and assisted living centers, dental offices, occupational therapy centers, cancer and medical research centers and eye clinics continues to escalate.

Generally, healthcare facilities want a soothing color palette. They avoid threatening subjects and like peaceful natural settings and landscapes. Recognizable portraits are usually not displayed, nor is abstract. Soft and uplifting subjects are desired. Prints are often acquired as they are less expensive and, if damaged, won't be such a loss.

Many hospitals also have programs where artists work with patients. Some even offer artist-in-residence opportunities.

HOSPITALS WITH ART COLLECTIONS

Community Hospital of Monterey Peninsula
www.chomp.org/pulse/2009/spring2009/Seideneck-art.aspx

The New York City Health and Hospital Corporation
www.artregister.com/nyc_hhc.html

University of Iowa Hospital and Clinic www.uihealthcare.com/depts/projectart

Yale/New Haven Children's Hospital www.ynhh.org/ynhch/ch_art.html

ART CONSULTANTS TO THE HEALTHCARE SECTOR

Aesthetics Inc www.aesthetics.net

American Art Resources www.americanartresources.com

Distinctive Art Source www.distinctiveartsource.com

Health Care Art Consulting www.healthcareartconsulting.com

ONLINE RESOURCES

Becoming a Corporate Art Consultant by Barbara Markoff
www.healthcarefineart.com/2009/11/how-to-be-a-healthcare-art-consultant.html

Picture of Health, A Handbook for Healthcare Art
www.henrydomke.com/PictureOfHealth.pdf

ORGANIZATIONS

American Art Therapy Association www.arttherapy.org

Art as Healing www.artashealing.org

Arts and Healing Network www.artheals.org

Arts in Healthcare www.thesah.org/template/index.cfm

Volunteer to bring art into the lives of hospital patients by having an exhibit, perhaps in a specific department.

Center for Health Design www.healthdesign.org

Healing and the Arts www.dms.dartmouth.edu/koop/programs/healing

International Arts-Medicine Assn/IAMA www.members.aol.com/iamaorg

International Expressive Arts Therapy Association www.ieata.org

Society for the Arts in Health Care www.thesah.org
The web site has a special resource section for artists to study regarding getting involved in the healthcare industry. They have a list of hospital members. They also hold an annual conference.

www.psychnet-uk.com/psychotherapy/psychotherapy_art_therapy.htm

HOTELS

The demand for art in hotels has increased expotentially in the last years. Some hotels are even titled "Art Hotel" (www.artfulhotels.com, www.artotels.com) as a destination hotel. A curator for a hotel often purchases for the bar, restaurant, guest rooms, front desk and lobby.

- When you travel, ask the concierge if he can give you the name of the art consultant who assisted the hotel in their collection.
- If you see the name of an artist on a hotel art piece, research her web site to see what consultant she worked with.

Art consultants working with hotels

Alexander & Associates www.corporate-art-consultant.com

Art Consulting Services www.artconsultingservices.net

The Art Group www.theartgroupllc.com

Art Initiative Inc www.artinitiative.com/

Art Scope Consultants www.artscopeconsultants.com

Artefact www.artefacthotelartconsultants.co.uk

ArtScape www.artscapeusa.com

Boston Art Consultants www.bostonartconsultants.com

Creative Art Services www.creativeart.com

James Roberston Art Consultant www.jrartconsultant.com

Joan Warren-Grady Art Advisory www.jwgaa.com

Kay Tiedt www.kaysartconsulting.com

Kevin Barry Fine Art Associates www.kevinbarryfineart.com

The Rosenberg Group www.rosenbergart.com

WINERIES

Wine and art seem to go together like a horse and carriage. Great collections within wineries are sprouting up all over the country. If you have the opportunity to show at a winery, make the most of it with help from the publicist for the winery. If you ever get the chance to explore the famous Napa Valley in northern California, be sure to plan a tour of some of the winery art galleries.

Di Rosa Preserve www.dirosaart.org
This collection includes over 1500 pieces from northern California artists from the 60s to the present. Installations, paintings, sculptures, scads of unusual creations.

Hess Collection www.hesscollection.com
Great collection of contemporary art

Quixote Winery www.quixotewinery.com/hundertwasser.html
Architecture by Hundertwasser

RELIGIOUS ORGANIZATIONS

Churches are traditionally patrons of the arts. Churches and synagogues utilize and display many works of art: murals, mosaics, stained-glass windows, sculptures, tapestries, paintings. The most active churches have separate foundations through which they can attract grants for art programming.

You do not need to be a member of a church or faith to create a work of art that is appropriate for them. You do, however, need to know that particular denomination's use of signs and symbols. Various colors also symbolize particular festivals and other celebration periods for individual denominations. The architectural style of the church, synagogue, or space, and the preference of the people involved will determine the size, color, and medium of artwork—the same as if you were selling to any other market.

Contact your local churches. If you can show examples of previous liturgical commissions, it would be quite helpful. If you have none, make some preliminary sketches of possibilities.

Memorials are often purchased by churches, so it is useful if they have your information on file.

- Contact architects who are building or restoring churches.
- Contact new churches being constructed in the area.
- Contact the regional headquarters of various denominations to find out about new churches being built that need artwork.

RESOURCES

The Spertus Prize www.spertus.edu/exhibitions/past/eternallight.php
A biennial competition for the creation of Jewish ceremonial art

Christians in the Visual Arts www.civa.org
They have an annual conference that features exhibits of art as well as workshops. They also have field trips, a newsletter and an artist directory.

Renting a studio space in a church is a practical idea—many churches have extra space, need the money, and want to assist artists. Perhaps you can even trade a piece of artwork for the rent. It can also become a great sales connection.

OUR LADY OF THE ANGELS

This new Los Angeles cathedral (www.olacathedral.org) was designed by Pritzker Prize-winning architect Jose Rafael Moneo of Spain. The previous church was demolished in the 1994 earthquake. This structure features 12,000 panes of translucent, veined alabaster (in place of the more usual stained glass) and 60,000 paving stones placed in a circular pattern centered at the altar. The tallest of the pipes in the organ is 40 feet high. Robert Graham designed the 25-ton set of bronze doors (30 feet high) as well as an unconventional sculpture of the Virgin Mary above the door. Lita Albuquerque created a water wall and fountain in the plaza. A guide to the vast amount of art in the cathedral is available at their kiosk outside the entry.

SMALL BUSINESSES

COUNTRY CLUBS

Country clubs need art for their club rooms, ballrooms, gift shops and dining facilities. If you create golf art, they are the perfect place for you to exhibit. Other types of art are well-accepted too. Country clubs can attract a good clientele, even if golf isn't your genre. They will sometimes rent out facilities for a show and let you use their mailing list of members.

- One artist in Florida has a show each year at his local country club. Each year he sells out. Can't beat that—and he's not a golf artist! Consistency, once again, pays off.

STORES

Consider selling to frame stores, art shops, print shops, department stores (gift departments), gift stores. Maybe an upscale boutique would be a good place to display and sell your work.

Bring order blanks, brochures and samples of work. Many stores will want artwork on consignment. Be sure to have a signed consignment agreement if you leave artwork. (Download a consignment agreement at www.artmarketing.com/downloads.html.)

An artist made a great deal with his prints of a local basketball coach when he connected with a car dealership. The company bought all the prints and used them as a giveaway with the purchase of each used car.

RESTAURANTS AND CAFÉS

Some artists have decided they would not hang their exclusive work at a café or restaurant. They are possibly missing out on a great venue.

One artist I know has a private opening annually at an upscale restaurant and sells out all the art on the first night. The works hangs for six weeks—a great promotion as she can leave her business cards, and the artwork has red "sold" dots for the entire six weeks. She has taken the time to build up this venue over the years and gets great local publicity from the local newspaper. Potential clients contact her to be put on the list for the following year's invitation.

INTERIOR DESIGNERS

Many artists don't consider interior designers to be buyers of art or reps of artwork. However, most interior designers have an eye for and love art. If they particularly like your art, they could be just the persons to get your career going. I know several artists who work exclusively with interior designers.

Interior design showrooms

In most major metropolises, there is at least one design center or showroom—a place where interior designers can shop at discounted rates for items they might need for a client. These can be great venues for an artist to exhibit at. The Blue Whale in Los Angeles is one such showroom. Online you will find a list of showrooms at www.i-d-d.com/interior_design_centers.htm and www.hollandandcompany.com/showrooms.asp.

Interior design events

Interior designers, especially high-end, are constantly looking for innovative items, so they often attend shows that are held across the country for the furnishings market. Some are Market Square, Hamilton Market and National Furniture Mart.

- For a list of interior design events, go to www.i-d-d.com/calendar_of_events/calendar_of_events.htm.
- Also check out International Home Furnishings Center/IHFC, High Point, NC www.ihfc.com.

Resources

The International Interior Design Association www.iida.org

American Society of Interior Designers/ASID www.asid.org
They publish a quarterly magazine for members called *ICON.*

Interior Design Magazine www.interiordesign.net

ARCHITECTS

Some art sales to corporations can be commissioned through architects.

Interior Design Society www.interiordesignsociety.org

Large architectural firms are divided into departments: engineering, architecture, interior design, graphic design, landscape design. To find architectural firms that are involved in current building and renovating projects, ask your public librarian for local publications that list new construction in your section of the city or county.

- *Dodge Reports* is a publication of McGraw-Hill. These reports list new construction plans, describe their scale, and note the architect in charge. A subscription is very expensive—$2000-plus. For this reason, not many libraries subscribe. Find someone in an architectural firm or construction company who subscribes, and arrange to read them at his office.
- Call the regional branch of the American Institute of Architects/AIA or your local Chamber of Commerce and ask for a list of architects in your area who specialize in commercial buildings.
- Make your own list of architects by looking for building sites. They generally display signs naming the architect.
- Speak or display at an architects' (or interior designers') gathering or luncheon. Make them familiar with your work and professionalism.
- Be listed in your local arts council's slide registry, where architects visit to locate artists for their projects.

Resource

American Institute of Architects/AIA www.aia.org

Building and property management

These large businesses construct and manage buildings and often decorate their lobbies with paintings and sculpture. They frequently know which of their tenants are interested in buying artwork for their offices. They might need to furnish a model home or apartment; if so, introduce them to your lease program. Try www.allpropertymanagement.com or www.npma.org.

Real estate agents

Businesses and private individuals tend to buy art when they relocate. Real estate agents can tell you who is moving where and whether their clients may be prospective buyers.

REAL ESTATE

Read the business section of your local newspaper for leads: where new companies are opening, where established companies are moving.

One enterprising artist put together a package deal that her local real estate company couldn't resist. She discovered that when a salesperson closed a sale, she gave the buyer an inexpensive print to hang in the new house or office. She put together several medium- and small-sized framed prints and sold them for under $50 to the real estate company. It worked so well that the artist and her husband took a booth at the state real estate convention and are now selling to real estate companies regionally.

Another artist teamed up with a sculptor and showed work in several new homes during a builder's opening.

Real estate developers

Developers put together all the aspects of a new building; they select an architect, contractor and designer. They need help! Find out what art consultants a particular developer works with, then contact them.

PUBLISHING AND LICENSING

Licensing is granting the right to a licensee—a publisher or manufacturer—to reproduce your artwork on a product in return for a fee or royalty.

If the style of art you create is widely accepted, you might be a candidate for the publishing and licensing industries. Within those industries are calendar publishers, poster publishers, limited-edition publishers, card publishers and manufacturers of articles on which art is printed: lunch boxes, aprons, shower curtains, pillows, t-shirts and more.

RESOURCES

Art Publishers Association/AOA and Photo Marketing Association/PMA have combined their resources. www.pmai.org

Artist's and Graphic Designer's Market www.artists-market.com

Art Business News www.artbusinessnews.com

Decor www.decormagazine.com

Licensing is a $170-billion industry, and growing; a huge increase from 25 years ago, when it was estimated to be a $10-billion industry worldwide.

Licensing is the business of leasing a copyrighted or trademarked "property," in this case a work of art, by means of a contractual agreement (a license), for a specific product (or promotion or service), for a specific time period, in an agreed-upon territory, for an agreed-upon fee or royalty.

Artists, illustrators and photographers have the opportunity to enhance their incomes and reputations by licensing their work for many products, including greeting cards, prints, posters, gifts, stationery, T-shirts, collector plates, furniture—literally hundreds of items. Licensing is an excellent way to build awareness nationally and internationally, thereby increasing the collectability of your art and, hopefully, the prices of your originals.

Museums, many of which frowned upon licensing in the past as "too commercial," are now licensing art in their collections—Monet, Warhol and Mondrian, to name a few.

For an individual artist, the question is, "How can I introduce my work to the licensing marketplace?" *Licensing Art 101* will guide you through that process by showing you how to study the marketplace and how to create effective presentations that focus on specific products and potential licensees.

Artwork chosen by licensees (publishers and manufacturers) must have wide consumer appeal and stand up against the competition. Licensees are looking for that "extra something" in a work of art that gives it broad consumer appeal. The more product that is sold, the higher the royalties that are generated for you, the artist.

❧

This article was excerpted from *Licensing Art 101* by Michael Woodward. www.licensingcourse.com michaelwoodward@mac.com. To purchase a copy of his book, go to www.artmarketing.com.

Chapter 11

The Portrait Market

Getting a commission

Initial consultation

First meeting

Sessions

The unveiling

Legal aspects

Resources

Pet portraits

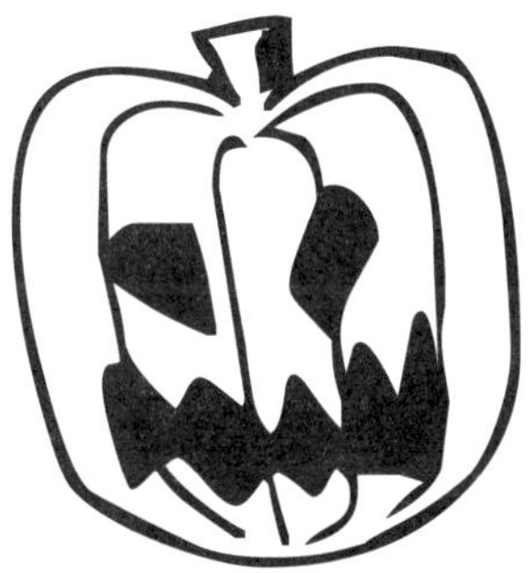

What the mind can conceive, it can achieve.

Napoleon Hill

GETTING A COMMISSION

Portrait commissions, be they of a pet, person or building, have been popular throughout time and are still thriving today. Here we will be talking about how to carry out a portrait commission in the most easily facilitated manner—so both parties end up with happy outcomes.

Before you agree to do portraiture, you'll need to decide whether you can and want to do commission work. Many artists are hesitant to accept commissions. Why? Because it means you will be told what to do. It means you have to deal directly with someone else's opinion. Will you mind that?

Contracts

- Sign a written agreement for any commission you schedule.
- Make sure the contract includes an advance for the cost of materials and part of your time.
- Determine what size, frame, coloring, and style might be best. Talk the client through your ideas.

Portraiture

- You need to make sure that your client enjoys the process of sitting and you enjoy the process of painting.
- You need to keep in touch with your client after the process. A quarterly postcard could lead to another commission in the future.
- See a sample portrait commission agreement at www.artmarketing.com/downloads.html.

Terms

The terms of a portrait commission are similar to other types of commissions. You will note what medium you will be using, what size, propose the scale of the figure (full or head), specify if it will have an abstract or detailed background, and set up a time schedule.

INITIAL CONSULTATION

In the contract you have sent them (details have not been filled in yet), you have already determined what the method of payment will be. I highly recommend the 1/3 (non-refundable) deposit upon ordering, 1/3 when approximately half finished (set a date), and 1/3 upon acceptance of final product.

You have chatted with the potential commissioner on the phone or in person, and she has told you she definitely wants to commission a portrait.

Set up a time in her home or office at least 7-10 days in the future. In the meantime, you send her information to browse. Ask her to review the information before the scheduled meeting. Let her know verbally that this initial consultation is part of the commission. Should she decide not to do the commission, the meeting will cost $____.

- This small fee prevents anyone taking advantage of your time.
- The 7-10-day lead time also gives her a chance to back out or postpone the commission should she change her mind after reading your literature.

Call her the day before the appointment to verify time and date. Reestablish that it is important that she's read and understood all the paperwork you sent.

If you will be doing a portrait of one or more young children, make sure the children are at this initial meeting. You will want to get comfortable with them before you take pictures in their most natural postures.

The packet you will send to the new client will include:

- Simple cover letter: a one-page letter explaining what is enclosed and what is expected of her
- The time schedule, according to what you've discussed on the phone (included in the cover letter
- A short introduction on how you work (included in the cover letter)
- Price and size sheet
- A portrait questionnaire
- Model release for her to sign (see page 138)
- Two copies of a contract; each of you will keep one. (Download a portrait commission agreement at www.artmarketing.com/downloads.html.)

Sample Price and Size Sheet

(You will have prices filled in.)

24x18; no background; one person $ ____ two people $ ____

24x18; landscape/interior background; one person $ ____ two people $ ____

24x36; no background; one person $ ____ two people $ ____

24x36; landscape/interior background; one person $ ____ two people $ ____

36x30; no background; one person $ ____ two people $ ____

36x30; landscape/interior background; one person $ ____ two people $ ____

Delivery and installation ________________________________

Framing ____

Frame

After you have personally determined what types of frames might look best, ask your client what type of frames she likes. If you agree, you won't have a problem. If you feel strongly she needs to review her frame choice, start now to talk with her about that. Don't expect her to change her mind right away. She will be paying for the frame separately (and perhaps purchasing it herself). If you want to leave that out, be sure it says in your agreement "unframed."

Sample Portrait Questionnaire

Do you have a particular idea in mind, setting, season, etc?

Would you rather let the artist decide the setting? Yes No

Do you want to be smiling? Yes No

Background: ❑ Plain ❑ Props ______________________

❑ Traditional ❑ Casual ❑ Modern ❑ Interpretive

❑ Vertical ❑ Horizontal ❑ Square ❑ Circular

❑ Indoor ❑ Outdoor

Particular colors or tones? ______________________________

Where do you want this piece to hang? ______________________

Size desired? ______

On the day you have scheduled your first meeting, your client should have answered this questionnaire, which you sent to him in advance. By glancing at it, you should be prepared to proceed with the meeting.

FIRST MEETING

Even though the client might have specific ideas about her commission, be sure to give your opinion. You are the artist, and you know more than she does about the best way to portray this person (even though she might not agree.) If you can't come to a mutual agreement, be sure you don't take another step in the commission process until you feel totally comfortable.

- Spending this initial time with the client will give you a feeling for her personal character. You will discuss finances at this first meeting and sign a contract.
- Bring your camera to this first meeting. You will be taking some preliminary photographs of the client standing, seated or in the position you think she might best be posed for her personality. Don't scrimp on the photos: 70-80 should be taken, both overall and for details of hands, face, props. By doing this, you have already started the process, and it is now harder for her to back out.

Tip

→ Be sure to ask why the client chose you. What did she particularly like about the piece that convinced her to hire you? Look at the other artwork in the client's environment: style, colors, genre. Is your style radically different from the other art hanging in her house?

Establish the parameters of the commission

- Size
- Type of clothing
- Objects included
- Formal/informal pose
- How much time will be required of your client for sitting
- Where the sittings will occur: indoor/outdoor, standing, sitting, etc.
- How long you will be painting after the sitting process
- Has she ever commissioned a piece before? If not, you will need to be careful to go over all details with her about how it works. If she has, find out how it went.
- Who is paying for this piece: Do you have to please more than one person?
- Inform her of your deadlines. You don't want to be rushed.

If you do portraits of children, let your local day care and children's museum know.

Ideally, it would be best to paint the portrait in the room and under the lighting where it will hang. Understanding the hanging position will be helpful.

The contract is finalized by signature by both parties and the down payment, which is stipulated in the portrait commission agreement you sent her.

- If she has excuses about payment at this time, expect to receive more excuses along the way.
- If she says she want to wait, save all the information you have gathered and ask for the fee for the first meeting (which you had explained during your first phone conversation).
- Accepting credit cards might help with any financial hesitations.

SESSIONS

PREP

The contract has been signed, a deposit has been received, and both parties have reviewed the pictures you took of the client(s).

- Choose five to 10 pictures—different poses, different props, different lighting—that you think would be the best basis for your portrait. More often than not, one stands out from the others and it is an easy choice. E-mail them to your client.
- Discuss ideas with her on the phone or via e-mail.
- Create a few B&W sketches.

SESSIONS

Depending on how you work, this initial portrait session (not the first meeting) with the sitter posing is the time to start doing a study, blocking in the features of the face and general background. If a child is involved, you have already requested the parent to attend.

- Bring your own lighting and props.
- When illuminating the face, have the primary source just off center so as to prevent strong shadows.
- For outdoor portraits, have the sunlight filter over their shoulders through their hair.

This first session will take approximately two hours. Always allow a little extra time; if you are slow, then allow three to four hours. If you finish early, she will be relieved! You can tell her it went smoother because she is such a good client.

You might have two or more sessions at the home; perhaps you work more privately. This has all been discussed pre-signing, so the purchaser knows clearly your methods.

You will also want to keep her informed during the process. Two or three digital photos sent via e-mail should satisfy this requirement. Ask her to comment on anything she might want to during this process.

Note about halfway through the development with an e-mail and a picture that the piece is approximately 50% completed. Politely remind her that a second payment is due. Until you receive this payment, do not proceed.

THE UNVEILING

If you have agreed to finalize the piece framed, make sure you have it framed when you deliver it.

The final presentation occurs not long after the e-mail you have sent with an almost-completed portrait. In this e-mail, arrange a time for the unveiling. Remind her politely that the final payment will be due at that time.

BE THEATRICAL

Wrap the piece in paper or cloth while you transport it, not only for its protection, but so she will not be able to see the final product when you arrive.

Show it to her by unwrapping it. This is your baby too. It might be best to show it only to the client you've been working with, not the entire family. You decide beforehand.

If the client has immediate criticisms, deal with her tactfully. Since you have been in correspondence with her, she shouldn't have a very complex problem. If that should happen, ask her to live with the painting for a week or two. Indicate that you will be glad to make changes at that time if need be. Converse with her by phone a week later. If she is still having a problem, arrange a visit. Try to make the changes on the spot while the client is watching. If not, take the painting back to your studio to work on it. If you leave the painting with her, you should collect your last installment.

SUZIE

The first portrait commission I helped with when I was an art rep was a great learning experience. I was a novice and had no book or person to guide me. I had no idea that a contract needed to be signed for this venture until later in the project. When I produced the contract (about halfway through the commission), it wasn't user-friendly. It was too full of legal jargon. The client cringed.

After we got over that hump, things went somewhat smoothly. I neglected, however, to show the progress of the painting to the client—the mother of the young girl in the portrait. It was before the time of e-mail and digital cameras, but I should have sent a photo. The final piece, thus, was a total surprise.

The mother mostly complained about the expression on her child's face; she was not smiling, and that's not how she envisioned her daughter.

I suggested she keep the painting for a couple of weeks and see how she felt then. It was a Renoir-style portrait, beautiful for anyone to own, not just the family.

I received a call from the mother some days after she had taken it into her possession. She had come to terms with the expression because she had found a photograph of her daughter in a dance class with the same expression! If that expression was on a photo, then it was okay in the painting!

LEGAL ASPECTS

Invasion of privacy act

If you execute a portrait of someone, be sure you obtain a model release for future use of this painting in your brochure, newspaper article, publicity, or sale at an exhibition. Without this release, you cannot reproduce it or exhibit it in public without possible threat of a lawsuit. Any failure to obtain such a release can be construed as a violation of the rights of privacy of the individual who served as the model. When the model is a minor, the written consent of a parent or guardian is necessary.

Models can object to altered images. If your model release form does not cover altered images, the model may bring an action under an invasion of privacy or publicity rights statute that enables the model to control the use of her name, likeness, voice, signature, or photograph in connection with the advertising of goods or services. The model need not show injury to reputation. Invasion of privacy doesn't apply after someone dies; however, an estate may have the right to all images of any given celebrity.

Celebrity images

Celebrities, athletes, and artists have certain rights in regard to the commercial use of their image, voice, or persona. You can paint anyone you wish and hang it in the privacy of your home. When it goes beyond that arena, however, there could be some problems even if you use an image of a deceased celebrity. Privacy rights extend to the celebrity status of deceased persons, and their heirs must give permission. The use of celebrity persona for satirical purposes falls outside the celebrity right to privacy, however.

The Marilyn Monroe Estate controls the image of Marilyn Monroe. When an artist executed a painting and had 5,000 prints made, the estate caught wind and took the artist to court. The artist tried to give the estate a royalty, but they would not accept the offer. The artist was told by the court to destroy all remaining prints. The estate personnel made certain this was done by going to the artist's studio and assisting him in destroying the prints.

❧

Another artist had a wonderful offer from an art publisher. The publisher wanted to reproduce the painting she had created by copying a photograph originally taken by a professional photographer. She called the photographer to find out if he would sign a release to allow her painted portrait to be published. Even when he was offered a royalty, he refused to give her permission. She had infringed on the photographer's rights by copying his photograph.

MODEL RELEASE

On _______________________________, I, __________________________________, posed as a model for artwork (to be) created by ____________________________________. In consideration of the payment of the sum of $ ________ at the conclusion of this modeling assignment, I hereby grant the irrevocable right to the use of my likeness in any and all media and in any and all manners including composite, segmented or altered representation for the preparation of works of art or any other lawful purpose. I hereby waive my rights to approval/rejection of the completed works which may incorporate my image, and hold harmless the Artist and the Artist's representatives against any and all liability arising therefrom.

I am an adult living in the State of _______________. I have read this model release and understand its contents.

Date ____

Model ____

Address ____

If model is minor

As Parent/Guardian of the above-named Model who is underage, I hereby consent to all the terms stated above and accept on behalf of the Model the consideration set forth above.

Date ____

Parent/Guardian ____

RESOURCES

ORGANIZATIONS

A Stroke of Genius www.portraitartist.com

American Society of Portrait Artists/ASOPA www.asopa.com

Portrait Society of America www.portraitsociety.org

Portrait Society of Atlanta www.portraitsocietyofatlanta.org

Portraits/Chicago Inc www.portraitschicago.com

Society of Portrait Sculptors www.portrait-sculpture.org

CONSULTANTS

www.portraitconsultants.com

www.portraitconsultants.org

www.portraitsinc.com

www.theportraitgroup.com

www.theportraitsource.com

COMPETITIONS

www.commissionaportrait.com/competition.asp

ARTISTS TO WATCH

www.baldwinfineart.com

www.janieemery.com

www.timothychambers.com

www.williamchambers.com

PET PORTRAITS

Display examples of your animal portraiture in a veterinary office.

Animal lovers crave portraits of their pets. If you create animal portraits, you have a huge, local clientele.

Tips

- Check out other pet or wildlife artists online to see what shows they've participated in.
- Create a win win situation with an animal organization: www.arthelpinganimals.com

Shows and competitions

International Exhibition on Animals in Art www.vetmed.lsu.edu/art_show.htm
A competition; one entry appears on the cover of *Journal of the American Veterinary Medical Association.*

Leigh Yawkey Woodson Art Museum Birds in Art www.lywam.org/birdsinart

Federal Duck Stamp Competition www.fws.gov/duckstamps/contest.htm

Conservation Stamp Competition, Wyoming Game and Fish Department
www.gf.state.wy.us/services/publications/stamp/index.asp

One artist-entrepreneur had a vision and made it come true. An animal portraitist, he created the nonprofit "Canine Companions for Independence," which brings physical assistance to children and adults who have lost the full use of their arms or legs. This nonprofit provides dogs that have been trained for two years to perform simple, everyday tasks that most of us take for granted. He combined forces with a leading store and direct mail marketer and now advertises pet portraits through this company—giving some of his proceeds to his organization.

Artists to watch

www.cwkrieger.com

www.intricateart.com

www.susanmorrison.com

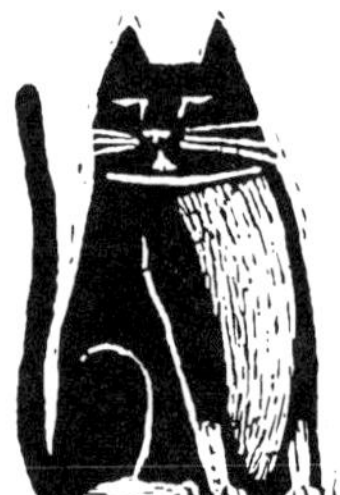

Chapter 12

Art Competitions

Entering competitions

Locating competitions

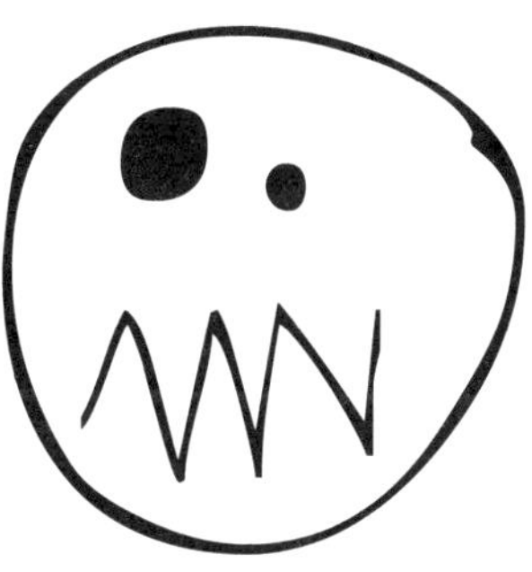

An exhibition doesn't begin when you enter a gallery, it begins the minute you get an invitation in the mail.

Mapplethorpe

ENTERING COMPETITIONS

Dali entered contests from the age of 12—and won most of them.

Competitions, both for emerging and established artists, occur quite regularly in all parts of the country. Many organizations, galleries and magazines sponsor competitions. A competition can be juried (with judges) or nonjuried (without judges).

The sponsoring organization generally charges an entry fee for a competition. Fees go to the production of the show, to the awards being offered, or to pay for the jurors. Jurors sometimes volunteer their time but most commonly are paid a fee.

Winning a juried competition is a prestigious accomplishment. Being juried into an exhibition can help you start building your resume. It shows gallery owners, consultants and collectors that people are reacting to your work. Gallery owners will be impressed by the entries on your resume that were judged by established members of the art world, so list the juror if you do win a competition. A winner of a competition could receive an exhibit, entry into a book or magazine, a monetary award, publicity, an article, sales or other awards.

- A competition can be a good way to gain public recognition.
- Competing can lend authority to your work and bring it to the attention of curators, critics, dealers and collectors who visit the exhibition.

Ask before applying

- The number of entries the previous year versus the number of works selected
- What percentage of last year's works sold?
- Is there a sales force on-site at the opening and throughout the exhibition?
- How is the show advertised to the buying public?
- Who pays for shipping if artwork is accepted?
- Who is the juror? Look in *Art in America Annual Guide* if you are not familiar with the juror's name. Perhaps you can find her listed there.
- Will printed price lists and information on artists be available to the public?
- What are the prizes?
- What was the attendance at previous years' shows?
- Are the works insured while at the show?
- Check with the Chamber of Commerce to see if they know the organization hosting the event.
- Where are the works displayed?

- Do all works need to be for sale?
- Entry fees?

ASK YOURSELF

- What do I want to get from entering this show: sales, recognition, exposure, something to write on my resume? Be sure the shows you apply to will fulfill your needs.
- Whether you win the competition or not, try to attend the exhibit. Why was your work not selected? Sometimes there is absolutely no way for you to know. Other times you can see that the jurors had a specific idea of what they were looking for—xomething very different from your style of work.

At Portland Museum in Oregon, the winners' works were hanging in the museum gallery. In a small room off to the side, slides were being shown of *all* the entrants' works, whether they were accepted into the show or not. This was very educational. Too bad it doesn't happen more often.

INSIDE THE JURY PROCESS

A jury seeks a consistent vision or aesthetic in visual work from an artist. Jurors judge on the basis of originality, craftsmanship, style, composition, inspiration. Samples of your work that are synergistic are the best choice for sending to a competition. They will have a stronger impact.

Generally, jurors sit in a darkened room with a note pad. They don't know the title of the piece, nor the artist's name. The juror only sees the artwork. All five pieces from the same artist are projected at the same time. What effect do they have together? Try it with your own slides and see!

- ★ Keep an inventory of what you send and where.
- ★ File applications not yet sent by the due date.

If you lose every competition you enter, it doesn't necessarily mean you aren't ready for the marketplace. I would suggest a consultation with an artist consultant if this happens; tell her the problem and see if she can find the flaw. Perhaps it is your presentation. Perhaps it is your style or subject matter. She can give you more guidance and, hopefully, direct you to better results.

★ Put yourself in a juror's shoes. If you were reviewing 3000 slides for a show, would you pick one of yours?

★ Look at your digital images. Are they clear, sharp, distinct, color-correct, powerful? To outdo 2999 other images, they have to be all that, as well as innovative, creative, and well-executed. If the piece is out-of-square, it indicates that the artist is not up to par on his photography skills. Such a flaw doesn't always eliminate a piece, but when something is awry it will invite more scrutiny. If it is too dark to view without squinting, it might be eliminated in a wisp.

LOCATING COMPETITIONS

To keep track of competitions you've entered, use the helpful worksheet "Competition Record" at www.artmarketing.com/downloads.html.

The classified sections of local and national art publications list many competitions, both regional and national. It's also easy to access competitions online.

www.artshow.com

www.artopportunitiesmonthly.com

www.artdeadline.com

www.artistsregister.com/opportunities.phtml

www.artdeadlineslist.com

www.NYFA.org

www.theartlist.com

www.artcalendar.com

If there are any local competitions of particular interest to you, mark them on your calendar so you can visit them to see the results of the jurying the year prior to applying. A preview like this will help you prepare for the next year's show. Keep in mind, however, that every juror is subjective, so styles and subject preferences change from year to year and juror to juror.

Apply to local shows first. If there is a competition elsewhere for a specific subject matter or style that you do, then extend your geographic limitation. If you are a watercolorist, check out that group online. Go national only after you have explored many shows, know a little about the history of any given show, and have won some local competitions.

Tips

- Be selective. Don't enter every competition.
- Museum competitions, or competitions with museum curators acting as jurors, can be a good introduction for your work to the museum world.
- Set a monthly limit on how much you are willing to spend to enter competitions.
- Read the prospectus carefully and follow directions.
- Shows that take a commission on sales are good; they then have initiative to sell.
- Read the information at www.artshow.com/juriedshows/entering.html.
- Read an article at www.graphicartistsguild.org/resources/guidelines-for-art-competitions.
- *The Art Opportunities Book: Finding, Entering and Winning* is available at www.artopportunitiesbook.com.

Competitions to consider

www.artkudos.com

www.ctacademy.org

www.midamericapastel.org

www.rosensculpture.org

www.christianartcontest.com

www.kingsleyartclub.org

www.paintamerica.org

www.utrechtart.com

Chapter 13

Art Fairs and Shows

Outdoor art fairs

Art trade shows

Open studio shows

Ignorance is not innocence, but sin.
Robert Browning

OUTDOOR ART FAIRS

Outdoor art fairs, if chosen wisely, can be a great sales venue for the emerging artist. Many people who are buying at these shows might be first-time art buyers, and a bit insecure. If they don't like your personality, they won't buy your artwork. It's that simple!

Working an outdoor art fair is not necessarily easy, but what is? Once you get the knack and find the right art fairs for your own artwork, you will see that they can be fun as well as financially rewarding. In fact, at some point you might be able to hire someone to help you. It is possible to make $1500-9000 and more per weekend. (If you are a smart marketer, there are after-fair sales too.) I know some artists who sell work priced at $9000 at outdoor art fairs. At the better art fairs, artworks from $1000-16,000 can sell. In order to receive these high prices, however, one must have a reputation and great presentation.

LOCATING AN ART FAIR

Local arts councils and art organizations often sponsor summer art fairs. Look in your local art newspapers.

ArtFair SourceBook www.artfairsourcebook.com

Harris List www.harrislist.com

Sunshine Artist www.sunshineartist.com

Art Festival Guide by Maria Aranjo www.amazon.com

CHOOSING THE RIGHT ART FAIR

The most important factor in having a successful art fair is choosing the right one for your art. Attend an art fair as a consumer. Ask artists how it's going. Get their business cards and follow up with a call after the fair. Be honest. Say you're calling to see if it's worth your while to show next year.

- Look for a show that is referred to as a "fine art show," not a craft fair.
- Are people carrying off packages? What are they buying—prints, originals, knickknacks, photographs?
- Do artists have red dots on their pieces?
- What style of art is being sold?
- What's the general atmosphere? Are artists happy? Sales up?
- What attracts attention at each booth? For example, monoprints priced between $50-250 sold like hotcakes at one art fair. Are your prices right for that fair?

OTHER ASPECTS TO CONSIDER

- How much does a booth cost?
- How many people are expected to attend?
- What kinds of sales has this art fair generated for past exhibitors?

- What happens in bad weather?
- What protection do you receive for displays left overnight?
- Can you demonstrate a creative technique during the art fair?

Download a "Show Analysis" chart at www.artmarketing.com/downloads.html.

Costs

Calculate your estimated costs—booth fee, motel, meals, gas, materials such as frames, shrink-wrapping, invoices, and business cards. Are all the expenses going to be covered by the price you are charging for originals and prints?

Applying to art fairs

As you begin to apply to the art fairs of your choice, you might find that the better fairs have a lot of competition. These art fairs are also juried, and artists from previous years may be given priority. To improve your odds of being accepted, you must remember that the judges are seeing only your reproductions, not your original work.

- Follow the prospectus instructions verbatim.
- Try to choose pieces that show the originality of your work, selecting subjects that are not frequently portrayed.
- Don't vary your style, medium or color too dramatically. Technical mastery is not what you are trying to show in your application. You are trying to emphasize overall effect of a particular style.

Acceptance

When you decide to apply to any particular art fair and are accepted, make it a goal to reapply for five consecutive years (providing, of course, that it was a good fair). You need to show consistency to the same customers each year. Create credibility. If you've researched and chosen your art fair well, you will have better and better results each year.

Rejection

If you are rejected, try to find out why:

- Was the number of applicants exceedingly high?
- Was it the quality or style of your work?

Most customers at fine art fairs are people who do not like to go into galleries. Many like to have a more personal connection to the artist from whom they are buying.

Before exhibiting at an art fair

- Create a mock-up of your booth and know what you are going to put where. If things change slightly during setup, that is fine; having a plan will save you time. Make a list of what you'll need to bring: picture hangers, stepladder, hammer.
- Have plenty of business cards, brochures, flyers and signs—all professional looking.
- Prepare short, precise answers to all the questions you can think people will ask you: How would you describe your work? How did you become an artist? Write these out on recipe-size cards and save them for periodic review.
- Make sure you personally invite any of your previous purchasers who live near the art fair.

Doing the art fair

So, you've been accepted to the number-one art fair on your list. Now you actually have to face the crowds. Your presentation could be the most important part of this fair.

Each art fair organizer will inform you of what type of equipment you need for exhibiting. Many artists use canopies, not only to protect their paintings but to protect themselves from weather elements. Some bring easels for displaying artwork. Generally, you won't have more than a 10x10′ area to display your work.

- Do you need a table and chair?
- What kind of backdrop will you display your work on?
- You will need a sales receipt book, perhaps some change, a large inventory of your work, printed literature, and a method to record the names and addresses of interested browsers.
- Be well-groomed. Wear comfortable shoes.
- Look friendly. Show enthusiasm. Wear a name tag.
- Open your booth; do not have the front of the booth blocked with tables or chairs. Make for easy access in and out.
- Have fresh breath and a good diet during the art fair so you will feel your best.
- Make your booth personal by having a bowl of candy available.
- Design a professional display that is lightweight and easy to install.
- Take time to eat, but not in the booth. Lots of art fairs have volunteer relief workers to give artists periodic breaks.

- If you have assistance from a friend, relative or mate, this lends support and relief. It's important to your mental health to rejuvenate and take breaks. People take energy to deal with. Some are very snooty, sassy, unintelligent, mean, nasty—all the adjectives we can think of. Remember, you are an actor and you are trying to deliver your lines the way you studied them.
- Trend-watch: walk the fair to check out the competition.
- Keep an even keel emotionally and physically.
- Make yourself available; do not sit in the back of the booth.
- Acknowledge visitors when they enter your booth with a short greeting. Start a conversation: "Do you collect art?"
- When pricing your work, write the price large enough on the tag so it's very easy to read. Why would you want to hide a price? Unusual pricing— $784— will show intention. If you've calculated the price to be $1034, it might be better to put it at $992 or something below $1000. Experiment and verify. Have a price range of items from $50 up.
- Label your work with price, medium if necessary, and "original" or "limited edition." This clarifies to the customer what he is looking at. Bring extra labels and price tags.
- There are yakkers and there are buyers: Watch the amount of time you spend with any given person.
- If two people are working the booth, never interrupt your associate unless requested. Let him do his own job. If you have a comment, save it for later.
- Display signs such as "Personal Checks Accepted," "VISA/MC/AmEx Accepted," "Free Local Delivery."
- Never break down your display until the fair has ended.
- Read *Selling Art 101.* Practice some of the scripts. Be prepared to sell, sell, sell!
- Plan to take two days off after the fair. Treat yourself to a massage or something relaxing, or you will come to hate doing them.
- Follow up with those people you said you would and whom you think could better your career.

Sometimes people don't know that they need or want something. It's your job to tell them why they want your art. Unless you know the benefits and believe in them, you won't be able to convince anyone else.

Sales are not the only aspect to consider at these shows. Finding a gallery or publisher could be part of your aim.

Supply check-list

- Business cards
- Brochures and giveaways
- Calculator
- Change/coins
- Guest book or signup sheet
- Inventory of work
- Packaging for purchases
- Pens
- Red dots for sold pieces
- Sales receipt books
- Sales tax certificate
- Table and chair

I went to the Sausalito Fine Art Fair about three hours after it started on the first day of a three-day event. One of the first booths I came to was a corner booth, set up very nicely, displaying pleasantly framed watercolor florals. The most prominent art piece had a red dot on it, indicating that it had sold. I thought, "Gee, already sold! Hmmm." I looked further in the booth and another piece had a red dot. I was really impressed; only three hours of sales time and two quality pieces had been sold. These pieces were in the $900-1200 range. I thought, perhaps, that she just placed these red dots on her paintings to make her look popular. But, as I was exploring her booth further, a man dragged his wife up to look at a $900 painting. They chatted a bit and decided within 45 seconds that they would buy the piece. Well, I realized then that this lady was for real. Her pieces had sold.

Dealing with people

All people walking by are potential customers. Treat them equally! Use no excuses: She's wearing clothes from K-Mart; she bites her fingernails; she can't have enough money for my artwork; it looks like he's tagging along with his girlfriend. When you start hearing yourself saying these things, it's time to take a break.

When someone is glancing for a while at your pieces, walk up casually and say jokingly, "Which one did you say you wanted shipped to your office?" Look at their reaction. Perhaps you want to add, "Or would you rather I deliver it and help hang it? I offer a variety of options—just let me know!" You're telling him playfully that you offer service with a purchase. He will like that.

ART TRADE SHOWS

Consider having prints made for ready-made frames for the $75-100 price range.

A trade show is where people in a particular trade—art, auto, buttons, cosmetics—set up a booth with products to show within that trade. There are quite a few upscale art-trade shows around the country: ArtExpo, Art Chicago, Art Miami, Modernism, as well as others worldwide. Most emerging artists do not exhibit at these shows. The mainstay of the exhibitors are high-end art publishers and galleries.

Sometimes, however, you will find established artists who are branching out into national exposure. These shows are no small event and need considerable planning and bucks. Booths generally run $2000 and higher. Transportation for yourself, your artwork, hotel and dining costs, setup at the show—all add up to thousands of dollars. Unless you are raking in the money and have a very specific plan with great sales people to bring in clients, you should not attempt this type of venue.

Scouting

As an active marketing artist, you should, however, attempt to *attend* shows as a *viewer*. You will make observations about marketing, brochures, displays, sales techniques and trends in the marketplace. You will also be able to learn what errors the exhibitors make in their presentations and how not to do the same.

THREE INNOVATIVE SHOWS

An artist who loved to paint orchids approached the producer of his local orchid trade show to rent a booth space. When the presenter found out he was an artist, not a grower, he refused to rent him a booth. The artist was determined, however, and explained to the presenter the possibilities for him. Finally, he was given a "test" booth. The test went off very well. The artist sold many orchid portraits and gained many new clients. He does the show annually now and has one of the most popular booths there. Take a risk! Go for it if you have a good idea.

What is a fine artist doing at an office supply show? He's taking a risk—a risk that turned out to be a good one! One artist decided to reach the business world by sitting at a booth in an office supply and furniture show. He was going to sell prints as well as originals, and possibly try to lease his original work to prospective clients. His main intent was to get names to follow up with after the local show was over. It worked. He became known within the business community in his area. Word gets around fast!

One artist started her career by showing and demonstrating at her local home show. It was a lot of tough work: setting up, sitting there for the entire weekend, dealing with people's comments. She decided that painting would be a good buffer zone for her, so she did demonstrations while the public watched. It worked well, and now she's gone on to bigger and better things.

Sales tax reminder: If an out-of-state client buys something and you ship it to him, no sales tax is charged. If this same client takes the piece with him, you must charge sales tax.

TOP ART TRADE SHOWS

Find a current listing of art trade shows at www.art-collecting.com/artfairs.htm.

Affordable Art Fair www.aafnyc.com

Art Aspen www.art-aspen.com

Art for the Home wwww.artforthehome.com

Art Hamptons www.arthamptons.com

Art LA www.artla.net

Art Los Angeles Contemporary www.artlosangelesfair.com

Art Palm Beach www.artpalmbeach.com

ArtExpo www.artexponewyork.com

Los Angeles Art Show www.laartshow.com

Miami Art Fair www.mia-artfair.com

Outsider Art Fair www.sanfordsmith.com

Philadelphia Art Expo www.octobergallery.co

Pulse www.pulse-art.com

San Francisco Fine Art Fair www.sffineartfair.com

Scope Art Show www.scope-art.com

FOREGIN ART TRADE SHOWS

Art Fair www.karaartservers.ch/art.fairs/netherlands.html

Art Show Zurich www.art-show-zurich.com

Barcelona www.fiac.com

Bologna www.artefiera.bolognafiere.it

London Art Fair www.londonartfair.co.uk

Scope Art Show www.scope-art.com

Toronto International Art Fair www.tiafair.com

OPEN STUDIO SHOWS

Publicity and your personal invitations bring potential clients to your studio at a set time on a particular day.

Opening their studios to the public is one of the most profitable ways artists these days are making a living. Building up a clientele in this way can create a large local customer base.

Citywide open studios

Citywide open studios—the type sponsored by a high-profile local art organization—report excellent sales throughout the US. Find out when a citywide open studio event is happening in your community and attempt to take part. Check your local arts council or organization.

If you don't think you have an appropriate studio, business patrons often let artists set up an exhibition in their facility. You could also collaborate with another artist and share her studio as well as expenses.

Even though the group sponsoring the citywide open studio event might be planning the publicity, you will need to do a lot of planning to make it a personal success.

Tips

- Have printed material for guests to take with them: a color postcard, business card with image of your work, a price list, all with your name, address, telephone, and URL on them.
- Emphasize tax deductions for business buyers. Artworks can often be deducted as office décor if the price is under $5,000.
- Have a special desk set up for sales purposes with sales invoices, flowers, and a chair on each side for completing the transaction.
- Hire a salesperson: Ask your local arts council for a reference or go to a local tourist gallery to find a part-time salesperson who wants to make some extra money; or, find a friend who's a good salesperson. Make sure you are comfortable with the salesperson's selling style—everyone is different. Educate the salesperson in detail before the event as to options for taking a piece on approval, lease programs, patron programs, and discounts for purchasing two pieces at the same time. Once the customer has decided to buy, tempt him to go on a buying binge by offering the companion piece at a 10% discount.
- Present various sizes and prices of pieces—prints if you have them, both unframed and framed. You want to hit all price ranges. Have one original piece priced high above the others.
- Mat reproductions nicely and personalize with a signature.
- If you frame your work, use the same style frame for all sizes. It will give more consistency to your work.

- Mark the price on each piece.
- When a purchase is made and the person plans to pick it up later, put a red dot sticker on its tag to indicate "sold."
- Have packaging materials ready in one corner of the room for carry-out purchases (bubble bags, tape, stapler). Perhaps you can get a friend to do this packaging for you.
- Be strong in all your statements. Create no doubts. Don't say anything negative about anything!
- Know when to stop talking. When someone is reaching for her checkbook, do not say another word. Let her say the next thing. Silence is golden at this moment. This is extremely hard for even good salespeople to remember!
- Get plates or mugs imprinted with your work. Do a search online for the right product.
- Do not get into a deep conversation with one customer. Many others will be floating through and you will miss them. People love to try to entice artists into a long conversation, but don't fall for it. Learn (and it does take practice) how to excuse yourself gracefully if this situation does come up.
- If nothing much is happening during your event, start moving your pieces around on the wall. See which looks best where. Ask some of your visitors. Get them involved. They'll love it! (See *A Science to Purchasing* on page 48.)
- Think carefully about the date(s). Consider your locale and other events that occur annually during any given weekend. Establish a date and stick to the same date annually. Mid-November and early May are good. One artist I know holds an open studio the first Sunday of each month.
- Give clients two days to choose from: Friday night and Saturday afternoon.
- Have a gala opening event, perhaps with a 10% discount or a free poster to draw people in. Create a memorable evening so they want to come back to the next event.
- Have snacks available. Be welcoming.
- Have excellent road signs for those who have never been to your studio.
- Make sure your parking areas are clearly marked.
- Invite your neighbors.
- Listen intently to all clients. They will actually tell you what they want.
- Practice makes perfect. Don't expect a sale the first time you start talking to someone. Build a relationship.

- Send postcards and e-blasts to your clients. A final-day reminder is a necessity too! Be sure to invite your dentist, doctor, pharmacists, grocery store clerk, and teachers of your children.
- Bring a stack of index cards and have people sign up for a drawing. Give away a print, a mug, a tile. This way you can get their address and e-mail for future communication.
- If someone talks about buying, yet is hesitant, offer an installment plan: Charge their credit card for three consecutive months.
- Have a goal as to how much you want to sell—a dollar amount. Work towards that goal. Your sales techniques will improve by having a goal.
- Make sure your choice of music is intentional. If you play Brahms lullabies, you might lull people to sleep.
- Give attention to all, but focus on the most active 20%.
- Some prospective clients are knowledgeable, while others know nothing about art. Be sensitive to the different levels of development.
- Do something different: Demonstrate your work, run a contest, have a story. Stories are fun—and your clients do want to be entertained. Stories should be short and to the point. Information is good. Tell them how a serigraph is made but keep it brief. Other customers need attention.
- Be yourself. Be prepared to give of yourself. Pay attention to constructive comments made by potential customers. On the other hand, don't heed the person who is expressing his vanity.
- Brace yourself for negative feedback. There's always a percentage of people who will criticize. Watch body language. You want your potential client to open up to you. Get him to unfold those arms.
- Make eye contact with your customers. They'll trust you more. Talk to people on their terms—no buzz words or art slang, just normal talk. If you use slang they don't understand, their egos will deflate.
- If transport of a purchase is a problem for someone who lives nearby, offer to deliver it for a small fee.
- When you decide to do a show, don't plan to party or socialize before. You need to eat, rest and relax so you can center your energies for the show day. It does take a lot of energy to spend the entire day "on the floor." Having a winning attitude is a necessity, and it's not easy if you're tired, hung over, or just not feeling confident.

Like a gallery, you want the level of excitement at your studio to be elevated.

- Have a theme. It could be related to the season, your new venue of art, or just something you like. Keep the theme year after year with slight variations. Part of your event could be a slide show about this theme.
- You can incorporate a silent auction into this event.
- If you have children or pets, find a babysitter outside of your studio for visitors. If a lot of your clients have children, arrange for a group sitter somewhere nearby, or, if your house is large enough, inside your house.
- Encourage people to sign your guest book so you can continue mailing to them.
- Greet everyone. Have a treat for each person or couple to take with them, something small but memorable.
- Send a thank-you note to any purchasers.

VALIDATE YOURSELF AND YOUR CAREER

You can gain the confidence of new clients by showing them which people and companies have purchased from you in the past. You are selling an overall appearance and "story." These locals want to know that you will be around for awhile. They want to know they are not being ripped off. They want to have their friends over to their home to show them the wonderful artwork they purchased. They want to feel confident about their art purchase.

- Create a portfolio you can set on a table for people to look through.
- If you have work exhibited in a book, display it on a table.
- Frame a magazine cover your artwork is on and hang it prominently in the entryway.
- If you've given to charity, make it clear: "Original artwork donated to Wildlife Foundation." This can be an icebreaker.

PRE-EXHIBITION OFFERS

One artist uses a pre-exhibition sale offer. When she sends out her first invitation for her show, she entices collectors to come to her studio for a private showing before the actual show date. She offers them a 10% discount. She also lets buyers know that she will be exhibiting the work they purchased throughout the entirety of the show. Thus, when her opening occurs, she will already have sold some pieces. You know how impressive it is to see red "sold" dots on pieces on the opening night of a show!

Giveaways

What one group of artists did, rather spontaneously, at a group show was to give away ceramic rats—funny-looking rat heads with comical noses and whiskers—that one of them had made. The artist was tired of storing them in her studio, so she made a sign saying that any sale over $50 (from any of the artists involved) qualified the buyer for a free rat. Every time a sale over $50 happened, an "aoooga" horn sounded and everyone cheered. The happy buyer was thrilled to have a gift. Soon, all 20 rats were gone (they were replaced with cat heads holding mice in their mouths).

Tip

- Check local magazines to see if there is someone who gives organized tours of artists' studios in your area. Sometimes museums do this. Try to become part of your town's art tour. In some communities, you can be listed as part of a cultural attraction. Consider forming a group with other artists who want to advertise specifically to tourists. Perhaps together you can produce a brochure to leave at all the tourist attractions, B&B's, hotels and motels in town. Contact your local Chamber of Commerce, museum or tour bus guides and introduce them to your studio.

Get feedback from your clients: What did they enjoy most about your open studio? Take that and use it to your advantage in the future.

7 WAYS TO KEEP CUSTOMERS COMING BACK

Service

In today's tight economy, personal service is the only way to survive! Spend more time with your client discussing color, texture, ideas—whatever is necessary to give him special attention. Follow up with a call to see how he's enjoying his new art piece. Talk to him.

Reminders

Send clients a postcard of your newest painting and let them know who purchased it. Collectors like to know that other people are buying your work. It makes you more credible. Send them invitations to openings you are having, even if they are far away. They want to know you're a success. Call to invite past clients to your opening. Remind them to bring their spouse, friend or business associate.

Toot your horn

Attempt to get press coverage in your area on a continuing basis. Collectors like to see your name in the paper and on TV. They want you to be a success because their investment will rise in value. They can say they helped discover a new artist.

Make it easy for the client to buy from you

Endorse a lease program. This is especially good for business clients. Start a Patron Program. Start a "Look Program" program that allows previous customers to "sit" with an art piece in their home or office for a short time before they finalize their decision to buy.

Stay organized

Don't forget people's names, what they purchased, what they like. Return phone calls, confirm appointments and follow up on every contact, referral and press coverage with a thank-you note.

Offer extras

Extra service builds goodwill toward future possibilities. Offer to hang the piece they purchased in their home or office. When you see their home, you will be able to make suggestions for other pieces that would complement their setting; many people need help in this area. Offer discounts for multiple purchases within a given period of time. Offer something special: customized framing suggestions, free delivery, home consultations, whatever it takes for them to value you and your artwork. They in turn will tell their friends, who will become great leads for future sales. Make it simple and easy for the customer. People who have money to buy art often don't have much time to spare.

Pay attention to your clients

This is the best way to know what to offer someone in the future. Most individuals are a reflection of many people's ideas and attitudes, so by listening to one person's views, you will be able to see what many people might want.

This article was written by Sue Viders and Constance Smith, authors of *Art Office*, available at www.artmarketing.com.

Chapter 14

Funding

Grants

Grant givers

Residencies

Moonlighting

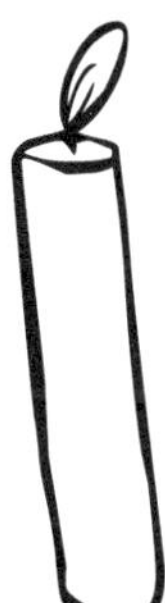

"Where shall I begin, your Majesty?" he asked. "Begin at the beginning," the King said, gravely, "and go on till you come to the end: then stop."

Alice's Adventures in Wonderland, Lewis Carroll

GRANTS

Grants should not be thought of as a primary source of income. In most cases, they are intended to assist an artist while she is becoming known.

A grant is an award of money, sometimes called a scholarship or fellowship. A grant does not require repayment. An individual, company or foundation sponsors a grant for a specific purpose or reason. Except for the research and writing time you need to spend to acquire the grant, you have nothing to lose by applying.

Researching grants

You'll need to have persistence, stamina and resourcefulness in your search for grants. If you don't research a grant thoroughly before you apply, you're wasting time and energy. Your aim is to find a grant that specifically fits your needs and your artwork.

Foundation center libraries

Foundation libraries carry books on grants. They are the best place to search for grant possibilities. (Your local library might also be able to help you find publications that list grants available to artists.) Books on grants will give you details on eligibility, deadlines, and requirements. Many grants are restricted to a certain ethnic background, geographic location, or religion; some are for study, some for travel. The five main Foundation Center Libraries are located in Atlanta, Cleveland, New York, San Francisco and DC. Each offers books, videos, live talks and seminars.
www.foundationcenter.org

Research pointers

- Keep your eye on grants for individuals, not corporations. *The Foundation Center's Guide to Funding for Individuals* is a good place to start.
- If the fund's name and the last name of the principal officer are the same, chances are it's a family foundation. They generally are smaller and more difficult to contact.
- The foundation library will have tax reports from each foundation. Check the IRS 990 Form of the grant giver you're interested in to see whom they gave grants to last year. Maybe it was given to their friends or family? Are they all from one geographic area, a certain age group, male/female?
- National art magazines often carry listings of available grants.

Find a funder that seems to fit your qualifications best and request an application.

Once you've narrowed it down to a list of three to five appropriate grants or fellowships for which to apply, you will need to fill out paperwork. Read the application packet carefully. Rethink whether this is the grant for you. When you have decided that it is, your proposal writing starts.

Grant writing

A grant proposal generally contains these parts:

Project Summary - One to two sentences that include the monetary amount of your request. Be specific about timeframe and amounts of money. Establish credibility and qualifications. For example: "The allotment of $5000 will be used in 2014 to print a catalog to be used for the Hoyt Museum exhibit."

The Problem or Need - The problem that receiving funds will resolve, as in, "I wish to make the most of having received a solo-exhibition at the Hoyt Museum in 2014. By receiving this grant for $5000, I will be able to print a quality catalog of my work, which will be sent to museum patrons, current customers and local art collectors."

The Objectives - The nature of the project. "The project is to include compilation and printing of a catalog of current work of my Hoyt Museum solo exhibit in June 2014."

The Method - How and by whom it will be done, as in, "Projected quote from designer through printer for 10,000 catalogs is $5000."

All aspects must be covered in detail and with certainty. Every word counts. You must write concisely and clearly. No rambling. Be direct. No lies. Write and rewrite this proposal. Leave time to edit and weed out unnecessary words. Make sure that you have communicated why your idea is especially worthy of funding.

You are not only writing this grant for the funding foundation, but you are writing it for yourself. You will come to understand your artwork and aims much more clearly once you have gone through this process. It often inspires new ideas and brings into your consciousness latent thoughts.

Grant-writing tips

- Have a well-written artist statement.
- Try to reach the head of the appropriate funding source.
- Know for whom you are writing this; who are the people on the committee?
- Usually a grant application will require you to limit your request to a defined space. Therefore, you need to make it as concise as possible. It should answer the who, what, when, where, why, and how of the funding request. If a question does not apply to you, write "N/A" or "Not Applicable." They will then know that you haven't overlooked a question.
- Don't philosophize. Be specific and clear in your request. If the panel can't decipher your concept, you'll be eliminated from consideration.
- Don't use jargon.
- Your application should be computer-generated. Use bold, italic and indentations to emphasize certain ideas. Be sure to have someone proofread the manuscript for typos.

Send a thank-you note if you are awarded a grant, to all levels of the foundation—the president, the secretary whom you spoke to many times on the phone. You will continue to send them cards and press releases—they are one of your best clients. If someone you've come to know goes to another agency, be sure to send her postcards and press releases at her new address.

- Follow directions precisely; keep your application neat, clean, and easy to read. Most grant guidelines request specific information in a specific format. Comply with all requests in the order requested. If a request is made for three letters of support, don't send five. If an applicant is not willing to follow directions in submitting an application, the grantor may question the applicant's ability to account for grant monies.
- Don't include promises that you can't keep.
- Make your numerical calculations clear, correct and easy to follow.
- Indicate what you hope to do and where the money will go.
- When itemizing your expenses, don't forget an artist's fee. You should be compensated for your time, not just for the material cost of the project. Factor in your time/labor as well as cost of materials.
- Send no extraneous material. Make it as easy as possible for the reviewer to "like" your request.
- Be positive. A chip on your shoulder will not get you a grant.
- If asked for work samples, send your best.

GRANT WRITERS

You can hire a grant writer if you don't want to write the application yourself.

- Some grant writers will also do preliminary research for your particular needs. They can save you hours of research time.
- They can provide you with assistance and inspiration and advise you on slide selection.
- They should be able to match your work with the foundations that will fund it.

LOCATING GRANT WRITERS

- Call one of the foundation libraries.
- Ask your local arts council.
- Contact a local Lawyers for the Arts organization. They often hold seminars on grant writing.
- www.grantwriters.net
- www.alliedgrantwriters.com

GRANT WRITING WORKSHOPS

Cause Effective www.causeeffective.org/resources/resources_workshops.php

The Center for Cultural Innovation ww.cciarts.org/bayarea.htm

Foundation Centers www.fourndationcenter.org

Kala www.kala.org

LegalArt Miami www.legalartmiamiorg

RECOMMENDED READING

The Complete Idiot's Guide to Grant Writing, 2nd Edition by Waddy Thompson

Grant Writing for Dummies by Beverly A Browning

MEETING WITH JURORS OF GRANTS

If you've passed the written proposal, the next step is meeting with the jury panel in person.

- Arrive early. Relax. Breathe deeply.
- Before your meeting, learn their names. Research their vocations and interests. Determine the key person(s).
- Plan your agenda to include three to five goals and key points, as well as an opening and summary. Thank them for the opportunity.
- State your objective and purpose, considering what they want to know.
- Conduct an interactive dialogue—no monologues. Establish eye contact. Their questions and your answers should comprise at least one-third of the presentation.
- Don't become defensive over objections that might be raised. If need be, ask for clarification of their question or concern.
- Remember, you are not selling anything; you are explaining a project you would love to be able to accomplish.

REPORTING GRANTS TO THE IRS

Most grants must be included in your annual income tax return. Only grants that meet one of the following criteria may be tax-free:

- Recipient is selected without any action on his part.
- Recipient is not required to render services as a condition to receive money.
- Amount of the award is transferred to a tax-exempt government organization.

A fellowship is an academic award, a merit-based scholarship or form of academic financial aid, often a residency with a stipend.

GRANT GIVERS

Try to find out before you apply if the grant is taxable. If it is, see if you can split the monies received—50% in one year and 50% in the next. Additionally, for your own personal accounting, it might be best to have monthly payments transferred to your checking account so you don't spend it all at once.

A Room of Her Own Foundation www.aroomofherownfoundation.org
Aaron Siskind Foundation www.aaronsiskind.org
Alabama State Council on the Arts www.arts.state.al.us
Artist Trust www.www.artisttrust.org/grants
Asian Cultural Council www.asianculturalcouncil.org
Craft Emergency Relief Fund/CERF www.craftemergency.org
Elizabeth Foundation for the Arts www.efa1.org
Flintridge Foundation www.flintridge.org
Foundation for Contemporary Arts Emergency Grants www.foundationforcontemporaryarts.org/grant_programs/immediate_needs.html
Franics Greenburger Foundation www.greenburger.com
Gottlieb Foundation www.gottliebfoundation.org
Guggenheim Fellowships www.gf.org/
Gunk Foundation www.gunk.org
Idaho Commission on the Arts www.state.id.us/arts
J Paul Getty Trust Fund for the Visual Artists www.getty.edu/grant
Judith Rothschild Foundation www.judithrothschildfdn.org
Legal Art Miami www.legalartmiami.org
Marie Walsh Sharpe Art Foundation www.sharpeartfdn.org
National Education Association/NEA www.nea.org
National Endowment for the Arts www.arts.endow.gov
National Foundation for Advancement in the Arts/NFAA www.nfaa.org
Pew Fellowships in the Arts www.pewarts.org
Pollack-Krasner Foundation www.pkf.org
Puffin Foundation www.puffinfoundation.org/grants
State Arts Agencies www.nasaa-arts.org
Visual Arts Sea Grant artdept@etal.uri.edu
Women's Studio Workshop www.wsworkshop.org

RESIDENCIES

Artists can find stimulation and a rewarding time attending a retreat or residency.

Residencies, art colonies, art communities and retreats provide opportunities free of distractions so an artist can focus on a specific undertaking in a serene and creatively supportive environment. They also provide a congenial atmosphere for the exchange of ideas with other artists. Most are free via an award grant. Some require a nominal payment.

18th Street Arts www.18thstreet.org
Alaska Residencies www.nps.gov/dena/supportyourpark/artist-in-residence.htm
Alden B Dow Creativity Center www.northwood.edu/creativitycenter
Alliance of Artists Communities www.artistcommunities.org
Anderson Ranch Arts Center www.andersonranch.org
Archie Bray Foundation www.archiebray.org
Arrowmont School of Arts & Crafts www.arrowmont.org
Art/OMI www.artomi.org
Atlantic Center for the Arts www.atlanticcenterforthearts.org
Bellagio Study Center www.rockefellerfoundation.org/bellagio-cente
Bemis Center www.bemiscenter.org
Byrdcliffe www.woodstockguild.org/byrdcliffemain.html
Centrum Foundation www.centrum.org
Colorado Art Ranch www.coloradoartranch.org
Delaware Center for the Contemporary Arts/DCCA www.thedcca.org
Dieu Donne Papermill www.dieudonne.org
Djerassi Residency www.djerassi.org
Dorland Mountain Colony www.dorlandartscolony.org
Edward Albee Foundation www.albeefoundation.org
Exploratorium www.exploratorium.org
Fine Arts Work Center www.fawc.org
George Sugarman Foundation Inc www.georgesugarman.com
Grand Marais Art Colony www.grandmaraisartcolony.org
Headlands Center for the Arts www.headlands.org
Helene Wurlitzer Foundation www.wurlitzerfoundation.org
Idyllwild Arts Foundation www.idyllwildarts.org/foundation.html
Jentel Artists www.jentelarts.org
Kala Art Institute www.kala.org
Kalani Honua Oceanside Retreat www.kalani.com
Kohler Art Center www. kohler.
Light Work www.lightwork.org
Lila Wallace-Readers Digest International www.wallacefoundation.org
MacDowell Colony www.macdowellcolony.org
Mapplethorpe Foundation www.mapplethorpe.org
Mattress Factory www.mattress.org
McColl Center for Visual Art www.mccollcenter.org
Mid-Atlantic Arts Foundation www.midatlanticarts.org
Millay Colony for the Arts www.millaycolony.org

Montalvo Center for the Arts www.montalvoarts.org
Montana Artists Refuge www.montanaartistsrefuge.org
New Museum of Contemporary Art www.newmuseum.org
New York Mills Art Retreat www.kulcher.org
Ox-Bow Workshop for the Arts www.ox-bow.org
Ragdale Foundation www.ragdale.org/residency
Sculpture Space Inc www.sculpturespace.org
Skowhagen School of Painting and Sculpture www.skowheganart.org
Snug Harbor Cultural Center www.snug-harbor.or
Split Rock Arts Program www.cce.umn.edu/splitrockarts
Stone Quarry Hill Art Park www.stonequarryhillartpark.org
Studio Museum in Harlem www.studiomuseum.org
Ucross Foundation www.ucrossfoundation.org
Vermont Studio Center www.ucrossfoundation.org
Virginia Center for Creative Arts www.vcca.com
Yaddo www.yaddo.org

Foreign residency programs

A number of opportunities exist for artists to travel and study abroad, with the assistance of a fellowship or scholarship to cover full or partial expenses.

American Academy in Rome www.aarome.org
This is the foremost American overseas center for independent study and advance research in the fine arts and humanities. It provides eight winners annually with a stipend, room, board, and work space. Located on 11 acres atop the highest hill within the walls of Rome, this is a very prestigious program.

Cité Internationale Des Arts www.citedesartsparis.net

Fulbright Fellowships www.fulbrightonline.org
Provides funding for a year of study and training overseas

US/Japan Creative Artists' Program www.jusfc.gov/creativeartists.as

Web sites

www.antiquesatoz.com/artatoz/grant.htm

www.artcalendar.com/article.asp?ID=214

www.artheals.org/artist_support/grants.php

www.artsfortheparks.comwww.americanartists.org

www.arts.ednow.gov

www.dir.yahoo.com/Arts/Organizations/Artists_Retreats_and_Colonies

www.iowaartscouncil.org/funding/grant-writing-tips.shtml

www.miraslist.blogspot.com

www.newyorkartists.net/art_grants.html

www.nyfa.org

www.unitedstatesartists.org

Recommended reading

Artists' and Writers' Colonies by Gail Hellund Bower

Artist Communities: A Directory of Residencies in the United States That Offer Time and Space for Creativity by Robert MacNeil

MOONLIGHTING

Wayne Thiebaud, a world-renowned artist, was a teacher for 30 years at UC Davis in California.

Besides selling your artwork, you may need to augment your income through some activity, hopefully art-related. This can lead to good connections and a supportive and nurturing artistic environment, and, possibly, clients for your artwork.

- Teach art at a college, through an adult education program, art organization, craft shop, art store, YWCA.
- Work at an art museum, art center, art supply store, gallery.
- Be a judge or juror for a show.
- Write a column for a local paper.
- Organize a lecture or slide show.

ONLINE JOB SEARCH

American Association of Museums/AAM www.aam-us.org

Artjob www.artjob.org

Artsearch www.tcg.org/artsearch

College Art Association/CAA www.collegeart.org/careers

New York Foundation for the Arts www.NYFA.org

NON-ART JOBS

Alternatively, you may wish to work in a non-art-related job, saving your art energy for your personal artwork. How about a waitress, typist, or bank teller? Working half days can get you in gear to go to your studio and work diligently in your off hours. You will value your time much more than someone who has all day free. I have seen artists get very confused and bored when they have all day to create. They really don't know how to do that. Being creative all day isn't easy.

INTERNSHIPS

Internships exist mostly in art organizations or museums. An intern may assist a director in a museum or art organization, or even another artist. Not only are you learning the trade, but you are meeting people, including potential clients. Some interns actually get paid!

VOLUNTEERING

Volunteering your time can connect you with local arts councils, art organizations, museums and other people who love art.

Chapter 15

Workshops and Travel

Developing a workshop

Speaking at a conference

Attending an art workshop

Art travel

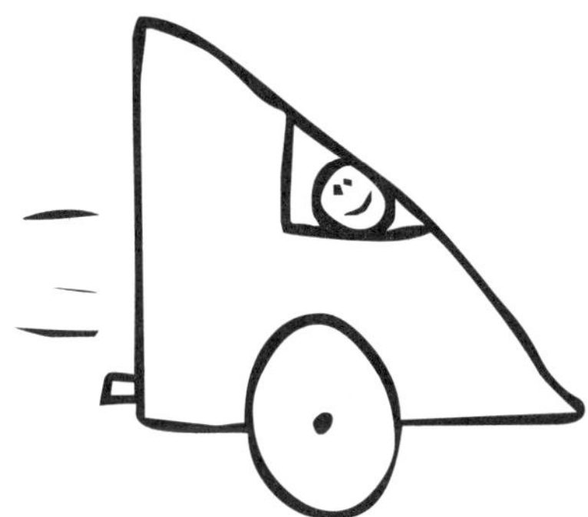

People often say that motivation doesn't last. Well, neither does bathing. That's why we recommend it daily. Zig Ziglar

DEVELOPING A WORKSHOP

Conducting a workshop is an excellent way to receive more exposure as an artist, as well as earn money. People who come to your workshop will have an opportunity to view your art and possibly become buyers.

Workshops are also great avenues for networking. When people have a common aim, they often bond quite easily, making for a pleasurable and intensive six hours or even a weekend. You will find that giving a workshop can be quite inspiring to your own creative juices. People are feeding off each other, circulating energies, and you're right in the middle.

What format do you want for your workshop: a few hours, an all-day event, a two-day retreat, a series of classes? If you haven't taught previously, it is better to start with a shorter event to get some experience under your belt. You will see if you like this venue, if it brings you what you want: recognition and income. Is it worth all the hard work? Are you comfortable being the leader?

When I first had the idea that I wanted to conduct marketing workshops, I began in the adult education system at local colleges. My techniques and materials got more and more refined. I learned how to handle an audience. I learned little things: taking a lunch break by myself was important, for example. Eventually I was confident enough to start marketing my seminars directly to the public. Since I knew my topic well, my presentations always turned out well—I satisfied the needs of the audience. It was a win win situation. I eventually formatted my notes into my first marketing handbook.

When and where

- Plan ahead: Give yourself at least four to six months of planning time. That way you can actually enjoy the process. You need time for PR, finding a space, designing flyers, outlining your program.
- Location is an important element. Your own studio or a friend's well-lighted garage might work fine. If it is a time of year when people plan to vacation, renting a spot in a retreat could be a good marketing idea.
- Give clear, written directions as well as a map to find the site.
- Know the maximum number of participants you can handle, both for the space and time you have. Ten students is often a good number for hands-on assistance.
- Is there access to water, bathroom, a stove? Let attendees know if they need to bring a sack lunch, drinking water or other supplies. Will you be offering coffee or snacks?

- If you plan to hold your class outdoors, be sure to have an alternate site in case of inclement weather.
- What will you need to bring? Start making a list and keep it for future workshops.
- Whatever you decide your workshop will teach, make sure they can learn it all within the given timeframe and that each attendee goes home with a finished piece of art.
- Part of any workshop is the social aspect. Make sure people interact as much as they need and want to. Make it fun. Each person needs some individual time; make sure they get it.

SOMETIMES BREAKING THE RULES WORKS

One time I planned a trip to Seattle around Labor Day weekend. Most people advised me I would not have attendees at a business seminar during a holiday period. Stubborn as I was, I decided to at least try and see if I could get 10 attendees. (Usually my maximum count was 15.) By golly! Those Seattle artists were thirsty for marketing information. They even came on a holiday weekend to my one-day seminar—15 of them! In fact, they really liked the idea that it was a holiday weekend because then they still had two more days off.

Who will attend

- Decide your target market. Make sure you note on the flyers what level of student you want to instruct: Do you want total novices to attend? Sometimes very experienced artists and novices don't mix; other times they do. You have to make sure it works if you are attracting both levels.
- Networking is vital. Talk about your workshop plans with everyone: "I am a workshop leader."
- Offer your workshop or class through continuing education programs at community colleges, adult education programs, community art schools, community centers, park departments, art supply stores, senior centers, women's centers, museums. You will need a detailed outline, resume, references, examples of your artwork and a supply list for your students. After you earn a reputation doing workshops for these community institutions, you can branch out on your own and possibly make more money.

For the fun of it, invite your best collectors to a workshop for a nominal fee (or for free).

Holding regular workshops—every other month—is to your advantage.

Make workshops a habit

Remember that the first time you do anything, it always takes longer and requires more effort than it will in the future. Once you get in the swing of promoting your workshop, it can become quite simple and routine.

Don't expect a great turnout the first time you promote a workshop. Word needs to spread, and will, if attendees have learned what they come for and are satisfied.

Creating a flyer

- Think of a catchy name for your workshop.
- Don't clutter the flyer with unnecessary information, only essentials—date, time, place, phone number, web site, cost, description of what you'll be doing, experience level required to attend, a short bio of yourself.
- After you do a workshop, get a testimonial from attendees and put at least one on the next flyer. People love testimonials.

Promotion

- Post your flyer at local cafés, schools, recreation centers, galleries, performance spaces, senior centers, grocery store bulletin boards—wherever it's legal.
- If people would travel to your workshop from a distance, find out ways to get PR further away.
- E-mail to your customers and friends.
- Use the US Postal Service to mail a card to a list of local artists.
- In addition to inviting folks you know, you will want to list your workshop in the community arts calendar and on Craigslist.
- Place an ad in your local arts council newsletter.
- Find a group of artists to invite you to do a demonstration at their next meeting, using this as a way to develop interest for your more lengthy workshop.

PUBLICITY

One artist I know creates her artwork while sitting in the window of her town's most popular frame shop. While she is painting, the gallery is displaying and selling her work. She has received word-of-mouth publicity as well as local media coverage. Buyers of art do love to meet the artist—and what easier way than this? This could be great publicity for her watercolor workshop too.

Pricing a workshop

The cost to attend your workshop should be calculated keeping in mind the present market value, demand, competition and your personal experience. Check out the prices of other artists online. One-day workshops (usually four to six hours) cost between $49 and $99.

Remember, you don't need a degree to teach art. Your experience and enthusiasm, as well as camaraderie with people, are enough for you to help and encourage others' creativity.

It's best to require full payment when registering. Artists need to make a commitment; you need to fill your class space as early as possible.

Create a syllabus

You will need to create an outline for the attendees, as well as a summary of what you will be teaching and how long you will be spending on each topic.

- If you are doing an ongoing eight-week course, three hours a week, have a week-by-week agenda of what you are covering to pass out the first week of class, and stick to it.
- If you have a web site talking about your classes—and you should—post the syllabus there to entice possible attendees.

Summary - "This course will cover a wide range of work related to advanced watercolor techniques. Students will practice drawing from observation, intuition and memory and will be encouraged to explore new methods." Look at the artists at www.watercolor-online.com to see how they describe their workshops. Another site to browse is www.watercolorsbyjanfoss.com.

Explanation - "Learning advanced techniques will take you to a new level of expertise in your particular style with watercolor. You will pick up tips from the other attendees that will help you keep your creative juices flowing into the new year. Competence will be practiced right on the spot."

Required materials - E-mail the list of materials to students before the first meeting. Keep it simple—items they already have in their studio. If there is something that is not easy to find and you want them to use this item, have it for sale or, better yet, charge a material fee that covers the item and provide it to them.

Presentation tips

- Practice.
- Arrive 15-30 minutes early so you can organize your materials and turn on the heater or air. You'll even have time to chat with early arrivals and not feel stressed.

Be creative in finding venues where you can speak:
interior designers' meetings
womens organizations
libraries
continuing ed
art supply stores
recreational centers
galleries
museums

- Start on time.
- Try not to fidget or say "uh" or "you know."
- Introduce yourself: who you are, how you qualify to teach this subject.
- Wear appropriate clothing.
- Use some form of visual aid.
- Take breaks every hour and a half or so; every hour in the afternoon if an all-day class.
- Bring some humor with you.

Speaking at a Conference

Being asked to speak at a conference is a privilege. As you advance in your art career, this opportunity will probably present itself. Sometimes you are offered a stipend, sometimes not. Of course, it is always nicer when you are paid for the time and effort. If you decide to do it pro bono, however, be sure you are compensated at least for travel and overnight costs, perhaps with a per diem rate.

No matter if you are one of many speakers or a keynote speaker, you will want to present your best. People attend conferences to learn, but also to experience. A good presentation motivates, teaches, inspires and creates memory.

Want do you want the audience to remember?

State this idea clearly at the beginning of your talk. Make your audience aware that it is *the most* important item they will take away with them. Other points you make will support this most important one. Instead of one main point, you can use three main points.

PowerPoint

Visual aids are always helpful to keep the audience listening. PowerPoint is the most common software program used for presentations these days. Learn it and use it—and keep it simple and focused.

Stories

Illustrate each important point with a story. This is what most people will remember—the example. Make sure the story makes a point. Keep the stories concise. A story can be as short as two sentences, but more often a few paragraphs.

Practicing

Once you have outlined your presentation (you will be told how many minutes you'll be allowed to talk), start practicing. Speak out loud in front of a mirror. Don't expect to become the confident voice within a few tries. Practice daily for at least two weeks. Try different inflections. What works best?

If this is going to be an ongoing experience (or if you plan to give ongoing workshops), you might want to work with a vocal coach. Even one lesson could make quite a difference and give you more confidence.

- Variation in tone is important.
- Variation in speed is helpful.
- Let important ideas linger in the air.
- Let emotional moments have space.
- Avoid um's, ah's; use silence.

- Your body shows a lot on stage. Our brains understand body language without any translation. Keep still; be intentional.
- Keep periodic eye contact with viewers.
- Breath deeply and evenly to keep relaxed.
- Take comfort in the fact that you are not alone with your nerves; famous actors often get stagefright. If your presentation is well prepared that will help relieve at least some of the anxiety.
- Visualize a contented audience during the weeks before your presentation.
- Think about your audience, not about yourself; it will help relieve nerves.
- Study other speakers.

Benefits of speaking

- Establishes you as an expert
- Brings additional income
- Builds up your audience of buyers
- Helps you keep current

Books

How to Run Seminars and Workshops by Robert L Joles
A thorough and well-organized book on the subject. Use it as a guide if you plan to develop this area of your career.

Fearless Presenting by Eric Maisel

Workshops are plentiful year-round both in the United States and abroad. It's a great way to rejuvenate yourself and your work. Decide what you can afford and where you would like to go, and start searching on the Internet or in art magazines.

US workshops

Art in the Mountains, Bend, OR www.artinthemountains.com

Blue Canyon Gallery, NM www.bluecanyongallery.com

Carol Marine Workshops www.bluecloudstudios.com/workshops.html

Ghost Ranch, Abiquiu, NM www.ghostranch.org

Websters World www.webstersworld.net

Foreign workshops

Abruzzi Mountains www.artworkshopitaly.com

An Artist's Life, Oregon and Scotland www.artistlife.com

Art in Amsterdam www.madebymeworkshops.nl

Artistvillage, Austria www.aon.at

Atelier Saint-Luc, France www.atelier-saintluc.com

En Plein Air, France www.pleinairworkshops.com

Giverney, France www.artstudy.com

Paros, Greece www.parosparadise.com

Plein air painting in Provence, France
www.ianroberts.us/workshops_provence.htm

Watercolor France, Italy, Frency Polynesia www.arttreks.com

ATTENDING AN ART WORKSHOP

Attending a workshop will teach you many things about your own potential workshop. Take notes on how it is run, what you like, what you want to mimic.

ART TRAVEL

2013 will bring a new book from ArtNetwork entitled Art Sites in the U.S.: Little Known Museums, Sculpture Gardens, Folk Art and Architectural Sites, a book that will take you to unusual venues that you never knew existed.. www.arttravelsites.com

Traveling while viewing art is one of the most inspiring ways to get refueled. There are a number of events, museums and inspiring art sites to visit throughout the US.

ART TOURS

Even if you're a "solo" adventure traveler, there can be some advantages to traveling in a group, especially when you all have something in common: art.

- Often you get to view private collections.
- You can see many art-related spaces in a minimum of time, with lots less effort than driving yourself.

Architectural Tours LA www.architours.com
Laura Massino, an architectural historian, takes you on the tour of your choice.

Art Immersion Tours of Florence www.florenceart.net/floart
Direct contact with artisans who explain their working processes and help you understand the beauty of traditional crafts. Awe-inspiring examples of "pietre dure" or hard stone inlay, gilding, decorative painting and silver beating.

Art Museum Council www.lacma.org/membership/ACArtMuseum.aspx
Art + Architecture Tour: View fine homes and private art collections in Los Angeles.

Art Smart www.artsmart.com
Art Smart is an art tour, travel and advisory company for the curious at heart. Whatever your interests, understanding or desires in art, they create engaging art experiences that are focused on you.

Chicago Architecture Foundation www.architecture.org
Many types of tours

Committee to Save Silverlake's Reservoirs www.csslr.org/newsevents/housetours.php
Annual one-day self-guided tours are organized to raise money.

Eyeopener Tours www.orangeshow.org/tours
Art-filled afternoons and weekend trips of creative exploring and one-of-a-kind experiences

Folk Art Society of America www.folkart.org
If you like folk art, joining this organization's annual tour can be very rewarding. They gain entry into many private collections. Their annual conference is held in a different city each year.

Garden Tours www.gardenconservancy.org/opendays
Help support the Garden Conservancy and visit private gardens in your area.

Glass Art Society www.glassart.org
Their conference is held in a different city annually with various private and public tours.

International Sculpture Center www.sculpture.org
Their symposium is held in a different city (and sometimes country) annually.

Museum guilds often sponsor tours to art-related venues, sometimes artists' studios or private collections: www.artic.edu/aic/calendar/events?EventType=1, also www.museumca.org/guilds.

Outsider Art Fair www.sanfordsmith.com/show.php?show=outsider
This art fair conducts tours to private collections.

Street of Eames www.streetofeames.com
Each spring this organization raises money for after-school programs for homeless and low-income children with a home tour celebrating mid-century and contemporary residences.

Overnights with Art

Anna's Bottle House www.bedbreakfasthome.com/raggtya
The bottle house almost defies description. It isn't round; it isn't square; it weaves this way and that, accommodating built-in seating, a platform bed, an elevated toilet, and a waterfall shower. The bottles range from clear Pepsi bottles to amber-colored beer bottles to green wine bottles. When the sun strikes them, the effect is quite beautiful. Included with the cottage is a large outdoor ramada that has a full kitchen, a sofa, another seating area, and an outdoor pool table with elephant legs.

The Art Cottage www.nevadacityvacationrental.com
The author of this book has created this retreat for the art-minded in the historic town of Nevada City, California. She exhibits and sells her art and creations to visitors within that environment.

Frank Lloyd Wright www.artmarketing.com/FrankLloydWright/links.html
A list of houses that FLW designed, some of which are available for short-term rental

Hotel des Arts, San Francisco, CA www.sfhoteldesarts.com
In this 51-room boutique hotel, guests receive an interactive experience—original art in their room, sometimes a mural on the wall. Each room is designed by a different artist (all can be viewed online). Along the corridors you will find artwork for sale. This hotel is not for the luxury-minded; the economic or student traveler will love it.

McMenamin Brothers www.mcmenamins.com
Throughout the Northwest, these brothers have been renovating old schools and buildings into hotels, restaurants, and pubs, keeping histories alive.

Foreign vacation rentals

European Villa Rentals www.rentvillas.com
Spain, Italy and France: great pictures to entice, with prices

Live Art Studio www.artfully.com/france.htm
Rent a space designed by an artist in a small village in France. Fun, fun, fun.

Paris Connection www.parisrentalconnections.com
Apartments by the week and month

Swapping homes

A great way to meet wonderful people, save money and travel like a native is to swap homes.

www.exchange.com

www.guestroomswap.com

ww.homeexchange.com

www.intervac.com

Recommended reading

Guide to Impressionist Paris by Patty Lurie
A beautiful four-color pocket-size book to take to Paris. Ms Lurie takes you on nine walks through Paris, accompanied by 80 famous paintings. The museum-quality reproductions are paired with color photographs of the locations as they appear today. Even if you don't go to Paris, this is a beautiful book to explore.

London Art & Artists Guide by Heather Waddell
Everything you need to know about the lively London art scene

*10 Steps to Getting your Sh*t Together* 28
80/20 rule 24, 48
25-25-50 rule 66

A

AAM 168
Abramian, Jackie 78
Abruzzi Mountains 177
Ad placement 66
  Artist directories 68
  Cardinal rules in advertising 67
Aesthetics Inc 119
Affordable Art Fair 152
AIA 73, 126
A L C Designs 88
Aldrich Contemporary Art Museum 81
Alexander & Associates 121
Allen Memorial Art Museum 113
Alyson Stanfield 21, 151
Amazon.com 30
America Business Info 62
American Academy in Rome 166
American Art Resources 119
American Art Therapy Association 119
American Association of Museums 168
American Institute of Architects/AIA 73, 126
American Society of Interior /ASID 125
American Society of Portrait Artists 139
Amit May Fine Arts 88
An Artist's Life 177
Animals in Art 140
Anna's Bottle House 179
Applying to art fairs 147
Apprenticing 64
Approaching a gallery 103
Architects 61-62, 72-73, 123, 126
Armstrong Prior Inc 88
Art Ability 88
Art Advice 88
Art Advisory 88
Art Advisory Services 88
Art and Business Council of New York 22
Art & Education 64
Art as Healing 119
Art Aspen 152
Art Business News 128
Art colonies. *See* Residencies
Art Concierge 88
Art consultants 28, 61-62, 70, 87-92, 116, 119, 121, 127
  Healthcare 119
  Hotel 121
  Portrait 139
Art Consultants Group 88
Art Consulting Services 121
Art Cottage, The 179
Art dealer. *See* Dealer, art
Art Directions 88
Art Environments 88
Art Exposure Inc 22
Art Fair 152
Art Fair Analysis 147
Art fairs and shows. *See* also Shows
  Applying to art fairs 147
  Choosing the right fair 146
  Costs 147
  Locating 146
Art Festival Guide 146
Art for the Home 152
Art Group, The 121
Art Hamptons 152
Art in America 66, 92
  Annual Guide 100, 142
Art in Amsterdam 177
Art-in-Architecture Program 73
Art-in-Embassies Program 73
Art Initiative Inc 121
Art-in-Public-Places Program 70
Art in the Mountains 177
Art LA 152
Art Los Angeles Contemporary 152
Art Marketing 101 7, 10, 13-14, 16, 18, 61
Art Now Gallery Guides 100
Art Office 90, 158
Art of the telephone, The 35-38
Art Opportunities Book 144
Art Palm Beach 152
Art Partnership, The 88
Art Pic 94
Art Plus 88
Art Publishers Association/AOA 128
Art reps 86-87, 91-92, 130, 136
Art Scope Consultants 121
Art Show Zurich 152
Art Source for Design 88

Bold type = Companies, shows and organizations

Art Source LA 88
A Stroke of Genius 139
Art Tracker 111
Art trade shows 151-152
Art Tribe 94
Art World Mailing Lists 62
Art + Service 88
Art4Business 88
Artaffair.com 30
Artconnect HQ 88
ArtExpo 151-152
Artefact 121
ArtFair SourceBook 146
Artful City 88
Artful Solutions 88
Artist Advocate 68
Artist Communities 167
Artist coach 20-21
Artist directories 68
Artist-Gallery Agreement 109-110
Artist in the Marketplace/AIM 22
Artist's and Graphic Designer's Market 128
Artists' and Writers' Colonies 167
Artists Circle 88
Artists Space 114
Artistvillage 177
Artjob 168
Artline 30
ArtNetwork 62-64, 179
ArtNews 66
Art/Not Terminal 114
Arts Advisory Service 88
Arts and Healing Network 119
Arts councils 70
Arts in Healthcare 119
Arts for Transit 74
ArtScape 121
Artsearch 168
Artsource Consulting 88
Artworks 88
A science to purchasing 48
ASID 125
ASOPA 139
Atelier Saint-Luc 177
Atlantic Gallery 114
Attending an art workshop 177
Attracting and Keeping Clients 53

B

Baker, Bob 21
Banking 28
Barbara Markoff 119
Barcelona 152
Becoming a Corporate Art Consultant 119
Benefits 45
Birds in Art 140
BizArt Conferences 22
Black Book, The 68
Blogging 29
Blue Canyon Gallery 177
Blue Tangerine Art 88
Bob Baker 21
Body of work 17, 32, 51, 107
Bologna 152
Boston Art Consultants 121
Branding 23, 116, 128
Branding Yourself Online 23
Breakfast Circle 21
Breaking the Rules 171
Brian Goggin 73
Broadcast media 78
Brochures 60
Brokers 86
Bromfield Art Gallery 114
Bronx Museum 81
Budget 25, 44, 51, 57, 63, 66, 71, 91, 116
Building and property management 127
Business of Art, The 22

C

CAA 168
Calendars 14, 26, 36-37, 78, 144
Calling tips 37
Calling Worksheet 35
Canine Companions for Independence 140
Cardinal rules in advertising 67
Care of artwork 49
Carey Ellis Company 88
Carol Dabb 88
Carol Marine Workshops 177
Caroline Stover 94
Celebrity images 137
Center for Education, Business and the Arts/CEBA 22

Italic type = Publications and videos

Center for Health Design 120
Certificates 52
Chamber of Commerce 24, 63, 99, 118, 126, 142, 157
Charity 156
Chicago Artists Coalition 114
Chicago Mosaic School 75
Chicago Public Art Group 74
Christians in the Visual Arts 123
Cityarts 73
Citywide Open Studios 153
Clear envelopes 59
Client Status Record 35-36, 118
Coaches 20-21
Collaborate 24, 73, 153
Collecting funds 63
Collectors Guide to Art of New Mexico 100
College Art Association 168
Commission 39, 50, 70, 73-74, 77, 86, 87, 92, 102, 105, 116, 123, 130-131, 133, 136, 144
Community Hospital of Monterey Peninsula 119
Competition(s) 32, 34, 42, 70-72, 73, 82, 90, 123, 128, 139-140, 142-144, 147, 149, 173
  Entering 142-143
  Locating 144
Competition Record 144
Competitors 34
Complete Idiot's Guide to Grant Writing, The 163
Conferences 22
Connect with the Buyer 96
Conservation Stamp Competition 140
Consignment Agreement 103, 124
Constance Smith 30, 158
Constant Contact 64
Consultants. *See* Art reps and coaches
Contemporary Artists' Services 102
Contracts 50, 80, 83, 86, 90, 94, 106-108, 117, 130-131, 133-136
Co-op galleries 42, 114
Corporate
  Art consultants 61-62, 87-89, 91-92, 95, 118, 121
  Collections 48, 166
  Gallery 47, 118
Coporate Artworks Ltd 89
Corporate market, The 116-118
Country clubs 124
Coupons 47, 52, 56, 59
Craigslist 30, 172
Creating Web Pages for Dummies 30
Creative Art Services 121
Creative Chicago Expo **22**
Credit cards 40, 44, 134, 155
Curatorial consultants 82

D

Davis, Mardine 94
Dealer, art *See also* Galleries
  45, 81, 86-87, 91, 98, 101, 107, 142
Dealing with people 151, 157
Defenestration 73
Design innovation 58
Design of promotional pieces 57, 60, 62
Developing a workshop 170-175
Direct Art Magazine 68
Direct mail 56-57, 60, 63, 140
Directory of Illustration 68
Discounts 47
Distinctive Art Source 119
Diversify 24
Di Rosa Preserve 122
Donations 70, 83
Dorsey-Hovde Art Design 88
Down economy 23
Downloads:
  Art Fair Analysis 147
  Brochures 60
  Calendars 14
  Care of Artwork 49
  Client Status Record 35-36, 118
  Competition Record 144
  Consignment Agreement 104
  Lease Agreement 49. 113
  Portrait Commission Agreement 130-131
  Press Release 78
DSA Fine Arts 88
Dvorák, Robert Regis 38, 53

E

E-mail 12, 28-29, 35-36, 64, 90, 95, 135-136, 172
  Blasts 23, 62, 64
  Newsletters 64
Easel Art Consulting 89
Educational TV 94

Bold type = Companies, shows and organizations

Effective Websites for Artists 30
Eflux 64
En Plein Air 177
Entering the Art Market 32-41
Entrepreneur 61
Envelopes, clear 59
Exhibiting art online 29-30
Exhibition 29, 39, 56, 61, 70, 74, 77, 79, 84, 86, 95, 102, 109, 117, 137, 142, 153, 158
  Announcements 59
  College 112
  Museum 81
  Solo 161
  Traveling 82

F

Facebook
  How to Sell on Facebook 28
  Social media 28
Factors to Success 12
Fairs. *See* Art Fairs and Shows
Fearless Presenting 176
Federal Duck Stamp Competition 140
Finding your voice 17, 132
Fine Art Resources 89
Fine Arts Advisory 89
Flavorpill 30
Flyers, creating a 172
Folk Art Society of America 178
Follow up 38, 41, 47, 79, 103, 118, 146, 149, 151, 158
  Calls 35-6
Foreign residency programs 166
Foreign vacation rentals 180
Foreign workshops 177
Foundation center libraries 160, 163
Foweler, Ralph 94
Frank Lloyd Wright 179
From a Gallery Owner's Perspective 111
Fulbright Fellowships 166
Fundraisers 76, 83

G

Galleries 98
  Approaching 103
  Artist-Gallery Agreement 109-110
  Co-op 42, 114
  Guides 100
  Legalities 108
  Meeting with a gallery owner 103-104
  Myths 98
  Rental 113
  Search 99-100
  Studio visits 106
  Understanding galleries 105
  University galleries 112
  Why Galleries Reject Artists 102-102
  Working with a gallery 107
Generate Buzz on a Shoestring 50
Geoffrey Gorman 20, 92
Ghost Ranch 177
Gift certificates 30, 52
Giveaways 124, 149, 157
Giverney 177
Goggin, Brian 73
Google
  Pay-per-click 30
Gorman, Geoffrey 20, 92
GotPrint 59
Grants 118, 123, 160, 164, 166
  Grant givers 160, 164
  Grant writers 162
  Grant writing 161-163, 167
  Reporting grants to the IRS 163
  Researching grants 160
  Workshops 163
Grant Writing For Dummies 163
Guarantee 19, 40, 44, 51, 64, 102
Guide to Impressionist Paris 180
Guidebook of Art 68
GYST 22

H

Handbook for Healthcare Art 119
Handling objections 44-45
Hand Prop Room 94
Harris List 146
Have a plan 23
Healing and the Arts 119
Health Care Art Consulting 119
Healthcare arena 119
Hess Collection 122
Hollywood Studio Gallery 94

Italic type = Publications and videos

Horejs, Jason 20, 111
Hospitals 119
  Art collections 119
Hotels 91, 117, 121, 157
How to Run Seminars & Workshops 176
How to Sell on Facebook 28
Hudson River Museum 81

I

I'd Rather Be in the Studio 51
IIDA 125
I'm on Linked In, Now What? 30
Indian Arts & Crafts Association 22
Innovation 58
Inside the Jury Process 143
Institute of Mosaic Art 75
Intending 14
Interior designers 28, 61-62, 91, 125-126, 173
  Showrooms 125
Interior Design Magazine 125
Interior Design Society 125
International Arts-Medicine Assn/IAMA 120
International Corporate Art 89
International Exhibition on Animals in Art 140
International Expressive Arts Therapy Association 120
International Interior Design Association 125
Internet 19, 28-30, 59, 61, 177
  Options 28
Internet 101 for Fine Artists 30
Internships 168
Invasion of Privacy Act 137
IRS Form 990 163
Isaiah Zagar 75
It's in the Mail 63
It's Liquid 64

J

Jackie Abramian 78
James Roerston Art Consultant 121
Jason Horejs 20, 111
Jean Efron Art Associates 88
Jersey City Museum 81
Joan Warren-Grady Art Advisory 121
Jobs 23, 86, 168
Joel Straus Consulting 88
Juried shows 142, 144, 147
Jury process 143

K

Katonha Museum of Art 81
Kay Tiedt 121
Keep Customers Coming Back 158
Kevin Barry Fine Art Associates 121
Kinzelman Art Consulting 89
Klein Artist Works 22

L

Laughingsquid 30
Lawyers for the Arts 162
Learning to sell 42-43
Lease Agreement 49, 113
Leasing 44, 49, 113
Legal aspects 19, 22, 32-33, 50, 90, 93, 107-110, 113, 136-137 163, 172
Leigh Yawkey Woodson Art 140
Lendrum Fine Art 89
Libraries, foundation center 160
Licensing 24, 61, 94, 110, 128
Licensing Art 101 128
London Art & Artists Guide 180
London Art Fair 152
Look program 156
Los Angeles Art Show 152
Los Angeles County Museum of Art 113

M

Magazines 128
Mailing lists 47, 56, 61-62, 70, 78-79, 90, 100, 109, 118
  Coding 62
Making sales calls 38
Mapplethorpe 141
  Foundation 116
Marc Pally 89
Mardine Davis 94
Maria Piscopo 89
Marilyn Monroe Estate 137
Marketplace Empowerment for Artists/MEA 22
Markoff, Barbara 119
McMennamin Brothers 179
Meeting with a gallery owner 103
Merchant status. *See* Credit cards
MFI Art Company 89
Miami Art Fair 152

Bold type = Companies, shows and organizations

Michael Woodward 128
Michelle Isenberg & Associates 89
Microsoft 116
  MicrosoftPro software 61
Model release 32, 39, 131, 137-138
MOMA/San Francisco 113
Moonlighting 168
Mosaics 75
  Organizations 75
Motivating 14
Mural Arts Program 74
Mural Conservancy of Los Angeles 74
Murals 74
  Organizations 74
Museums 18, 22, 28, 32,44-45, 61-63, 74, 76, 81-84, 92, 86-87, 95, 99-100, 113, 140,143-144, 157, 161, 166, 168, 171, 173, 178-180
Museums of the World 82
Myths about galleries 98

N

Napa Valley Museum 81
National Society of Mural Painters 74
Networking 18, 21-22, 28, 60, 76, 86, 112, 117, 158, 170-171, 178
New American Paintings 68
New York City Health and Hospital Corporation 119
New York Foundation for the Arts 22, 168
Newark Museum 81
Newsletters 64
Niche markets 33-34, 39, 101, 111
Nonprofits 23, 75
  Working with 76-80
NYFA 22, 144

O

Official Museum Directory 82
Online Marketing Tactics 30
Open Studio Press 68
Open studio shows 12, 56-58, 61, 79, 96, 108, 153-154, 157
Openings. *See* Exhibitions
Orange County Museum of Art 81
Our Lady of the Angels 123
Outdoor art fairs 42, 45, 146-149
Outsider Art Fair 152
Overwhelm 26

P

Paros, Greece 177
Patron program 44, 50-51, 153, 158
PDF 28
Peak Fine Art Services 89
Pepsi 116
Percentage-for-the-Arts Program 70, 77, 87
Pet portraits 140
Philadelphia Art Expo 152
Phillips, Renee 46
Philly Magic Garden 75
Photo Marketing Association/PMA 128
Picture of Health, a Handbook for Healthcare Art 119
Pleiades Gallery 114
Plein air painting in Provence 177
Portland Art Museum 113
Portrait Commission Agreement 130-131
Portraits/Chicago Inc 139
Portraiture 130-140
  Commissions 130
  Contract 130-131
  Questionnaire 131-132
  Unveiling a commission 136
Portrait Society of America 139
Portrait Society of Atlanta 139
Postcards 12, 47-48, 50-53, 56-59, 76, 79, 99-100, 130, 153-154, 158, 162
  Deck 59
  Inventive 59
  Printers 59
Power Up with PR 25, 78
PowerPoint 175
Pre-exhibition offers 156
Precita Eyes Muralists 74
Presentations 151, 172
  Tips 173-174
Press release 30, 78-79, 99, 106, 130, 162
  Sample to download 78
Price and Size Sheet 131-132
Pricing 23, 42, 92, 148
  Workshop 173
Private collectors 87, 95
Professional assistance 22
Programs
  Look 158
  Patron 44, 50, 153, 158

Italic type = Publications and videos

Promo pieces 55
Promotion 21, 39, 42, 46, 51, 56, 59, 63, 66, 76, 81, 86, 124, 128, 172
Publicists 86
Publicity 53, 71-72, 78, 80, 83, 117, 124, 137, 142, 153, 172
PSAs 78
Word-of-mouth 67
Publicly-funded programs 70
Public Art Network/PAN 72
Public speaking 172-175
Publishing 128
Pulse 152

Q

Quixote Winery 122

R

Ralph Foweler 94
Real estate agents 127
Real estate brokers 127
Receptions 56, 82, 102, 104
Referrals 34, 38, 40, 47, 67, 95, 106, 158
Rejection 10, 12, 18, 106, 147
Religious organizations 123
Renee Phillips 46
Rental galleries 113
Renting mailing lists 62
Reps *See* Art Rep and Coaches
Researching grants 160
Residencies 165-167
Foreign 166
Resistance to success 11
Restaurants and cafés 124
Resume 47, 81, 142-143, 171
Risk 11, 18, 24, 26, 39, 49, 51, 60, 66, 97, 102, 151
Robert Regis Dvorak 35, 38, 53
Rosenberg Group, The 121

S

St Johns Cultural Art Center 22
Sales techniques 42-53
A science to purchasing 48
Handling objections 44-46
Saltman Art Associates 89
SAM Gallery 113
San Francisco Fine Art Fair 152
Sausalito Fine Art Fair 150
Science to Purchasing, A 148
Scope Art Show 152
Scripting important calls 38
Sculpture parks 74
SEA Conferences 22
Selling 42-48
Selling Art 101 35, 38, 53
Selling Your Art Online 28
Seminars 22, 162
Set decorators 93-94
Show Analysis Chart 47
Shows 145 *See also* Art fairs
Slide registries 70-71, 126
smARTist Telesummit 22
Smith, Constance 30, 158
Social and Public Art Resource Center, The 74
Social media 28
Social Networking for Artists 28
Society for the Arts in Health Care 120
Society of American Mosaic Artists 75
Society of Portrait Sculptors 139
Software program for artists 111
Speaking at a conference 175
Spertus Prize 123
Standard Rate and Data 62
Stanfield, Alyson 21, 51
"Starving" to Successful 111
Stover, Caroline 94
Studio sales 107
Studio visits 106
Prep 95
Subject lines 64
Success 10-13, 15, 18, 21, 23, 26, 31, 40, 46-47, 51-52, 56, 80, 84, 92, 107, 153, 158
Success as an Artist 22
Successful mailers 56
Successful Selling 46
Sue Viders 158
Sunshine Artist 146
Support system 32
Suzy Locke and Associates 89
Swapping homes 180
Syllabi 173
Sylvia White 21,101-102

Bold type = Companies, shows and organizations

T

Taking a Risk 60
Target group 63
Target market 33
Telephone, the art of the 35-38
  Etiquette 35
  Follow-up call 36
  Important calls 38
  Scripting important calls 38
Telling is not selling 53
Testimonials 57, 172
Thank-you notes 39, 47, 53, 79, 155, 158, 162
Think outside the box 12
Third time's a charm 57
Tone of voice 36, 53
Toronto International Art Fair 152
To Tweet or Not to Tweet 28
Tours 75, 116, 157, 178-179
Trade shows, art 151-152
Travel 121, 160, 166, 172, 175, 178-180
Traveling exhibitions 82, 84
Tressa Miller 89

U

Understanding Galleries 105
University galleries 112
University of Iowa Hospital and Clinic 119
Unveiling a portrait commission 136
Using the Internet 28
US/Japan Creative Artists' Program 166

V

Vacation rentals 180
Vertical Response 64
Vick Corporate Art Advisors 89
Viders, Sue 158
Visual Arts Advisory 89
Visual Arts Consultants 89
Visualize Success 11
Voice 13, 17, 32
Volunteering 168

W

Ward-Nasse Gallery 114
Warm calls 38
Watercolor France, Italy, Frency Polynesia 177
Ways to expand your clientele 39
Ways to Keep Customers Coming Back 158
Web site 12, 21, 23, 28-30, 34, 36, 56, 58, 60-61, 67, 92, 100, 177-178, 120-121, 172-173
Web Site Innovation 29
Websters World 177
Wendy Kelley Art Advisory 89
Who is attracted to my artwork? 33
Why galleries reject artists 101-102
Why we buy 48
Wineries 122
Woman Made Gallery 114
Woodward, Michael 128
Word-of-mouth advertising 67
Workbook, The 68
Working with a gallery 107
Working with nonprofits 75
Workshops 169-173, 177
  Fliers 172
  Pricing 172
World Innovators 62

Y

Yale/New Haven Children's Hospital 119
Yes! 48

Italic type = Publications and videos

BUSINESS BOOKS FOR ARTISTS

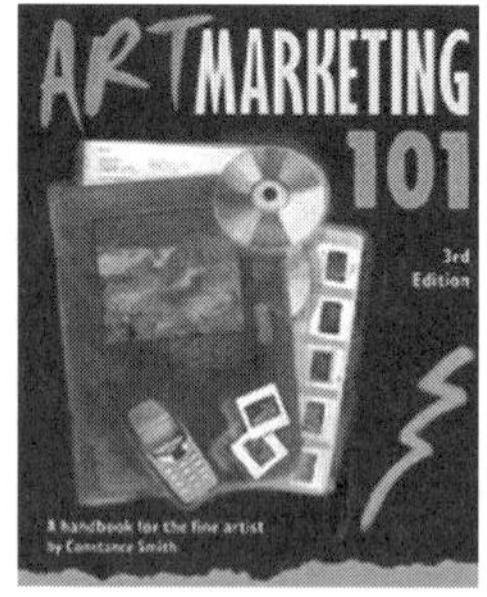

Art Marketing 101: A Handbook for the Fine Artist

This comprehensive volume covers everything an artist needs to know to market his work successfully. Artists will learn how to avoid pitfalls, as well as identify personal roadblocks that have hindered their success in the art world.

Preparing a portfolio * Pricing work * Planning an exhibit
Taking care of legal matters * Developing a marketing plan * Accounting
Resumes * Creating an artist statement * Secrets of successful artists

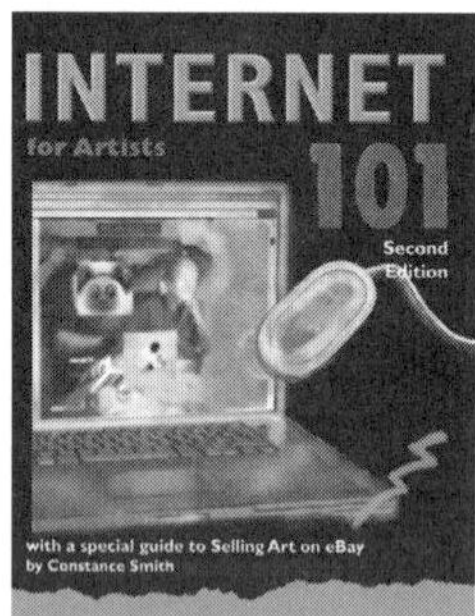

Internet 101 for the Fine Artist

This user-friendly guide explains exhibiting, promoting and selling artwork on-line.

Internet lingo * E-mail communication shortcuts * Acquiring a URL
Tracking visitors * Creative research on the web * Designing your art site
Doing business via e-mail * Meta tags * Search engines
Attracting clients to your site * Pay-per-click advertising

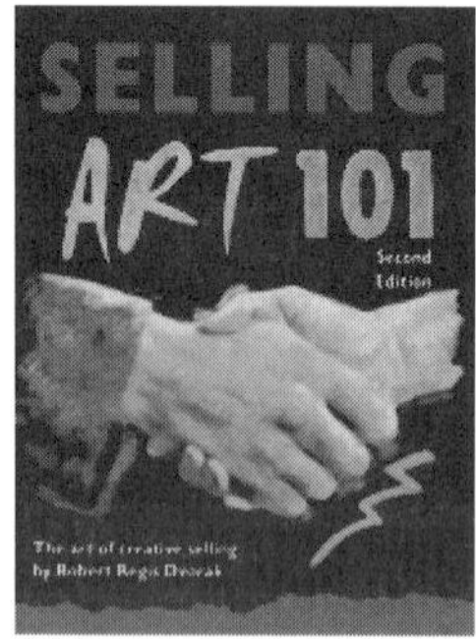

Selling Art 101: The Art of Creative Selling

This book teaches artists, art representatives and gallery sales personnel powerful and effective selling methods. It provides easy-to-approach techniques that will save years of frustration. The information in this book will take sales to new heights.

Closing secrets * Getting referrals * Telephone techniques
Prospecting and keeping clients * Developing rapport with clients
14 power words * Studio selling * How to use emotions
Goal setting * Overcoming objections

WWW.ARTMARKETING.COM